Kim & Axel Himer

Leather Care
Compendium

For Shoes · Clothing · Furniture

Type set in Zurich BT

ISBN: 978-0-7643-4517-3
Printed in China

© 2011 Heel Verlag GmbH

Das große Buch der Lederpflege: Schuhpflege – Bekleidung – Möbelpflege written by Kim & Axel Himer was originally published by © Heel Verlag GmbH.

This book was translated by Ingrid Elser.

Published by Schiffer Publishing, Ltd.
4880 Lower Valley Road
Atglen, PA 19310
Phone: (610) 593-1777; Fax: (610) 593-2002
E-mail: Info@schifferbooks.com

For our complete selection of fine books on this and related subjects, please visit our website at **www.schifferbooks.com**. You may also write for a free catalog.

This book may be purchased from the publisher. Please try your bookstore first.

We are always looking for people to write books on new and related subjects. If you have an idea for a book, please contact us at proposals@schifferbooks.com

Schiffer Publishing's titles are available at special discounts for bulk purchases for sales promotions or premiums. Special editions, including personalized covers, corporate imprints, and excerpts can be created in large quantities for special needs. For more information, contact the publisher.

Kim & Axel Himer

Leather Care
Compendium

For Shoes · Clothing · Furniture

Schiffer Publishing Ltd.

4880 Lower Valley Road • Atglen, PA 19310

Contents

Nicola, Axel and Kim Himer.

Acknowledgments

After four years of research and development for this book, we would like to express our thanks to several people. First of all, we have to mention Fabian Pfister, who significantly helped us with research and maintenance of the vast database. We are especially grateful for photographer Barthold Stromeyer, who enabled us to produce the book in this form. Without his picture compositions, we would not have been able to impart this work to the reader and viewer in a reasonable way. Furthermore, we thank graphic designer Bernhard Siegle for a layout well done. Appreciation to Nada and Horst Lichter for introducing us to agent Dr. Jürgen Pütz. We thank him for his great commitment from the very beginning and for believing in the idea of our book. Without him, we would never have come to Heel Verlag. Franz-Christoph Heel and his coworkers, especially our editor Sabine Arenz, are very much appreciated for their trust in us and for the liberties we had during the creation of this book.

Our gratitude is extended to all of the companies mentioned in this book for their support. Many thanks to Prince Asfa-Wossen Asserate for his well-disposed preface. Our thanks go to the following persons in particular: Attila Aszoti, Liz Buffo, Michael Baggeler, Jörg Beckhaus, Thimon von Berlepsch, Rainer Brüssow, Mark Fisher, Ingo Fischer, Ottmar Gerberbauer, Johann Glöckle, Peter Heinrichs, Patrick Hofmeister, Jürgen Hingsen, Michael Kober, Blanka Krieg, Frank Marrenbach, Jochen Mass, Adolfo Massi, Ralf Möller, Elmar Nyhuis, Ali Peneck, Prof. Dr. Erich Pfister, Dr. med. Siddharta Popat, Erol Sander, Christian Schims, Guido Graf von Spee, Carmine Tortora, Andreas Weiss, Nicol & Dirk Westendorf, Senator Dierk Wettengel, Ulrich Tröger, Oliver Wickert, and Tina Himer. And last but not least we thank Nicola Himer, sister of Kim and daughter of Axel Himer, for her participation and support during the creation of this book.

Foreword by Dr. Prince Asfa-Wossen Asserate

Besides wood, stone, and wool, leather is among the oldest materials used by humans. No wonder, because tanned animal skin is a very robust and versatile material. In former times, even parts of weapons were made of leather. Nowadays, above all, everyday consumer goods are made of this natural material.

Leather was the first material upon which humans wrote down their history. The significance and utility of leather has played a salient role in numerous facets of daily life since the first days of humankind. The natural product leather deserves natural treatment as well as processing. Leather appears to us as a second skin. Patiently it takes the shape of the artist's personal expression. Soft and tough in character, long-lasting leather is appreciated for its smoothness. Wearers as well as users know this from experience and become participants in a symbiosis with the leather. Together they go through thick and thin. The greater part of the leather produced worldwide is probably used for shoes. For the production of one shoe, different kinds of leather with totally different qualities are required.

Whoever looks at their feet has to be ready to come down off their high horse, has to make himself/herself small, to bend down, to become humble. This is not always easy, because it necessitates showing humility, which in turn requires a certain greatness.

One's feet are our contact with the ground; with our feet we move through our lives. Therefore, protecting them is unavoidable, and it is also unavoidable that this protection, which we call "shoe," becomes stained and dirty. On our path through life we also come into contact with impurity. The earth's dust and mud clings to our feet and quite often it was turned into a symbol for the impure and sinful.

For Muslims, Hindus, and Buddhists, as well as for Ethiopian Christians, it is customary to remove one's shoes at the threshold to a sacred place as well as at home. This way impurities are more or less left at the doorstep. In the Bible, this thought can be found as well at the point where God says to Moses: "Take off your sandals, for the place where you are standing is holy ground." The cleaning of shoes has a special meaning in many Oriental cultures, and in my Ethiopia as well. Everywhere in the cities you can find young people with their small stools and wooden crates in which they keep the utensils for cleaning shoes. The Ethiopian shoeshine boys are still called "Listros," a name that can be seen as a heritage from the times of Italian occupation between 1935 and 1941. In these countries, shoes have a good life because they surely are treated much better than in many European countries. A reason for this may be that having one's shoes cleaned is very cheap and everybody can afford this daily service. A model for the "service-related desert of Germany?"

As with any material, leather can be damaged by constant use. This kind of damage includes tears, abrasions, spots, disfiguration caused by snow, etc. Quite often you can also find cracks in the surface that can be caused by too much dryness as well as a too high a fat content in the leather.

Now Axel and Kim Himer, both designated experts with respect to leather treatment, have written a book on leather care. They have been remarkably successful in making this complicated subject clear and understandable to non-experts. Numerous tips and tricks on how leather objects ought to be treated are revealed. You will definitely not be doing yourself a disfavor by getting this book "under your belt."

For several years now I have known Axel Himer as a versatile and "restless" craftsman, who managed—together with his wife Tina—to pass their knowledge on to their daughters Kim and Nicola. They also strive for excellence and seek to set new standards in a dying craft. In the meantime Kim Himer has advanced to one of the best in her trade. The fact that father and daughter have now created *The Leather Care Compendium* as a joint project, I see as a landmark in our time.

—Dr. Prince Asfa-Wossen Asserate
Management consultant, bestselling author,
and political analyst

Introduction

The invention of a multitude of tanning procedures that turn animal skins into leather is one of the greatest achievements of humankind and is already several thousand years old. Only by means of tanning did it become possible for humans to settle in all the climate zones of the world. Compared to this, it is quite astonishing that professional leather care products were only developed about one hundred years ago. These modern leather care products not only maintain the value of high-quality leather items, but very often also provide enhanced functionality under the hard conditions of cold, heat, moisture, and abrasion.

During our twenty-five years of work as Kim and Alex Himer, Cologne, we constantly dealt with all kinds of leather and their care. Even the best type of leather has a longer lifespan if it is cared for properly. The word "right" has to be taken very seriously, because the wrong care and the wrong products can damage leather. Thus, it is important to use the right means for each "nursing case." Time and again we have been asked by our customers and the participants of our leather care seminars about the best methods and the best means for leather care.

Given this interest with respect to shoe and leather care, it is all the more astonishing that so far no professionally qualified literature on the topic has existed at all. To us, it almost seems as if in the wake of our society having been turned into a throwaway society, the knowledge about shoe and leather care has been thrown away as well. While two generations ago every child learned how to clean shoes at their family home, nowadays not even most parents know how to take care of shoes. Who still knows the difference between an emulsion cream and a hard wax paste or knows how to remove various stains or chewing gum from leather?

To bring some order into the chaos and to put an entire line of business—which at the moment is mostly ignored and wrongly so—back into the limelight, we decided to critically combine all our practical knowledge about leather care with the literature on the subject in our library to write this book. Leather furniture, clothes, shoes, saddles, accessories, and cars deserve good care. Finally, today, the best care products that ever existed are available to everyone. Using them to take care of a pair of comfortable shoes or gloves you cherish will not only be easier for you after reading this book, but will also provide for their long lifetime, good appearance, and prolonged value. In addition, you will feel an inner satisfaction about your own craftsmanship. Nevertheless, it is still a bit of work, as is revealed here. But, supplied with the right tools for leather care, this work has almost a meditative nature.

In this book, we introduce the tools and proper leather care products with which we achieved the best results during the past decades of our work. All the products and techniques are of high quality and we can recommend them without reservation. Of course, this is our subjective choice, with no claim to be complete, but it nonetheless gives a broad overview.

Having said this, we hope to provide good guidelines on leather care to the readers, by means of which they will maintain their shoes and other leather products better, and with more joy. If this is the case, we have achieved our goal.

Leather—the Indispensable Natural Product

Despite our modern way of living and our advanced civilization, leather, which is one of the oldest materials known to humankind, is much more a part of our everyday life than ever before. Never before have the means of its production, the diverse sources of origin, and the possible uses of leather been so multifaceted.

Leather was used by humans for clothing and the production of shoes since Neolithic times. Leather was also used quite early for creating simple homes, e.g., tents—not only by nomads living in steppes areas, like Mongolia where wood is scarce, but also in North American forest regions. No wonder, if you take into account that leather has a three times better heat insulation than oak. This is made possible by the air cushions embedded into the fiber structure of the leather. This means, one gram of leather tanned with vegetables has an inner surface of up to 980 square feet [300 square meters]. Prior to the invention of parchment, which is made from untanned hides, ancient civilizations not only wrote on papyrus, but also on leather. The Roman Empire provided its legionaries with armor made from leather; the Inuit covered their boats with leather until the beginning of the twentieth century. Chairs, armchairs, and couches were and still are covered with leather because of its elasticity and resistance to tearing. Bracelets and braided leather strips are used for ornamentation.

With the rise of printing in the mid-fifteenth century, a totally new use arose. Leather could be the best of all materials as a cover when bookbinding. Here even one type of leather found its use, which nowadays makes you shudder, leather made from human skin. In England, for example, the case record of a murderer was bound in his own skin after his execution. Luckily, leather was, and still is, of far greater importance in more joyful areas, e.g., as cover material for drums and in sports nowadays as material for the production of soccer balls.

When Hernán Cortés invaded what is now Mexico, at the beginning of the sixteenth century, the art of leather processing and decoration, in which the Spaniards were leading at that time, was brought to the new world. The educated Spanish leather craftsmen, who were responsible for the production of saddles and harnesses for the horses they had brought with them, came into contact this way with the impressive Central American flora, which in turn was reflected in the beautiful floral motifs of the decorated leather. Thus, a transition of the rigid geometric- shapes of the Late Middle Ages towards more pleasing, flowing shapes occurred.

Leather soles of a mountain-hiking shoe from 1870 with manually forged heel and sole nails.

For countless accessories and functional products, like belts, handbags, wallets, knife sheaths, watchbands, and saddles, leather is the first choice. Even in the bathroom, leather has established itself in male hygiene in the shape of the razor strop.

The use in cars, not only as leather seat cushions, but more and more as cover material for the dashboard and ceiling, seen historically, is still quite young, but quite important with respect to quantity. By the way, it is very interesting that leather as a material used in automobiles has already undergone a radical change of its appreciated value. For example, a Bugatti Royale was the most expensive and exclusive automobile during the 1920s and '30s. Its cabin was provided with expensive textile seats while the chauffeur had to sit on cheap, wear-resistant leather seats. Nowadays, in contrast, manufacturers of luxurious cars try to outdo each other with the quality and choice of their leather, and it is not a rare thing that one has to pay the price of a mid-class car just for an exclusive all-leather outfitting of such a limousine.

Today, 5.9 billion square feet [1.8 billion square meters] of leather are produced each year; about 65 percent of the skins are from cattle. Roughly 80 percent of that leather is used by the fashion industry for clothes, accessories, and—most of all—for shoes.

Despite all modern materials, new textiles, and artificial leather invented in the last one hundred years, the qualities of leather— with its unique combination of elasticity, tear resistance, insulation against heat and cold, ability to breath, low flammability, and resistance to wear—are not reproducible. Especially, its low flammability and wear resistance led to the monopoly of leather with respect to protective wear and gear for motorcyclists, which is still a hot topic and will probably stay this way indefinitely. Leather provides a multitude of top features and thus almost always is first choice among materials.

"Dirt Separator at Rendenbach." In the reeling machine, the hides are cleaned of salt, dung, and blood residues in warm water at 86 degrees Fahrenheit [30 degrees Celsius].

Leather—the Indispensable Natural Product

Custom-made shoes from a stingray.

Western saddle from cow leather.

Bentley Azure II, 2010 model, the convertible of the Arnage series.

izard, caiman, ostrich, and leather watch straps.

A Small Leather Lexicon

Leather is created by the tanning of hides and furs. By means of tanning, they are transformed into a permanent, durable state and are prevented from rotting. The body coverings of big mammals, like cattle, horses, or pigs, are called skin—like the ones of reptiles, fish, or amphibians. With smaller mammals, like sheep or goats, and, of course, all animals with dense, thick hair, they are called fur.

The skin of mammals consists of three layers: the thin cuticle (epidermis) with hair, sweat glands, and sebaceous glands, the thick dermis (corium), and the hypoderm (subcutis), which consists of the subcutaneous connective tissue and embedded fat cells. For the production of leather, only the dermis is suitable, which consists of the upper dermal papillae and the thicker reticular dermis with its bundles of fibers (fibrils).

The number of tanneries in Europe is shrinking, as is the amount of produced leather, because of ever more restrictive laws designed to protect nature.

Nowadays most leather is produced in India and Asia, and it is processed there as well, because leather, apart from a few exceptions, is not an end product. With respect to the often laborious, manual processing and low wages, Asia has an advantage as well. In Europe, tanneries are mainly working in niche areas or the luxury market.

The main tanning procedures are chrome tanning with chromium and mineral salts, vegetable tanning (also called pit tanning), chamoising, and synthetic tanning with aldehydes, acrylates, and phenols. Quite often various procedures are combined in order to influence the qualities desired of the finished leather. The exact combination of the tanning substances used is the secret of each tannery. About eighty percent of all the leather produced in Europe is chrome-tanned, about twenty percent vegetable-tanned, and only one percent is chamois-dressed. Almost all the leather used for clothing and shoes is chrome-tanned. Leather for furniture and cars is also mostly chrome-tanned, but is increasingly tanned with methods free of chromium (vegetable or synthetic tanning). High-quality leather for soles is always bark-tanned (vegetable). In the following pages, the most important methods for tanning are described.

"In the making of the leather, the stink is what holds it together. Lime, alum, flour, arsenic, and salt make it white and pretty without fault. Egg yolk, sausage, and dog shit give the quality to it. This is a flavor you won't miss; give the glove a tender kiss."

—Ancient Tanning Rhyme

Chrome Tanning

Chrome tanning with mineral salts exists since 1958. Today it is the tanning method most commonly used.

"Dry storage" at the Rendenbach tannery. Prior to hanging up the already tanned leathers for drying, they are treated with a special vegetable oil.

The first step toward a high-quality product is already made by the choice of raw materials. Skins from cows and calves are waste products of slaughtering houses, where they are bought by business people who, in turn, trade them. These hide dealers sort the goods they bought by gender and weight and conserve them by curing and cooling. A coarse cutting to size is also done. After that, the raw material is sold to tanneries and leather manufactories.

The first production step is soaking the hides in a big rotating drum as part of the so-called "beamhouse operations" prior to the actual tanning process. During this first step, the hides receive back their initial water content by means of soaking. In addition, they are cleaned of salt and dirt during this water bath. After that, the hair is removed during "liming" with lime and sodium sulfide. During this work step, which takes thirty hours approximately, proteins and fats are washed out of the skins. The result is the "pelt," as the skin freed from fur is called. Now follows excarnation, with the removal of the connective tissue from the pelt and the first cut to remove legs and tail. Then the pelt is cut with a knife into grain split and flesh split. The grain split, also called top grain, is used for upper leather; the flesh split is used for split leather, which is further processed into leather for linings or suede leather, sometimes also into gelatin.

Upper leather raw hides are cleaned in the barrel.

Here, the colors are prepared for the Hoffmans tannery.

are used. Both tanning methods take up to twenty hours to complete. In the samming machine, the leather is dehydrated between two felt rolls. Afterwards, it is cut lengthwise and sorted into quality categories according to its thickness, its scars, and the number of visible mosquito bites. In a barrel for dyeing, the Wet Blue is neutralized and freed from the residues of the tanning acids. Then, during retanning and dyeing, fresh tanning agents and colors are added in accordance with the customer's wishes. This way pre-determined parameters, such as color, grip, resistance to tear, and elasticity, among others, are achieved. High-quality leather stays in the dyeing barrel until it is thoroughly dyed. At the conclusion of the process, the desired softness is reached by adding fat.

By means of adding hydrophobic fat, water-repellent leather is created that is nevertheless able to conduct water vapor and sweat to its outside, providing the perfect

Now actual tanning takes place. It is also done inside big, rotating drums. First, during deliming, the split is freed from lime; during bating, collagen is reduced by means of tanning agents with added enzymes in order to prepare the skin for absorbing as much of the tanning agents as possible. In the following pickling process, acids (sulfuric acid and formic acid) are added together with neutral salts in order to lower the pH-value. Only then are the actual tanning agents added. Mineral tanning is mainly done by adding salts of trivalent chromium, aluminum, and iron. During this process, the small chromium molecules settle down well within the fibers and pores of the hide. By adding brine during the so-called basification, the chromium particles expand and thus anchor themselves to the hide. This process of bonding of tanning agent and hide is the actual tanning; skin has been turned into leather by now. The freshly tanned, still moist leather pieces have been dyed blue by the chromium. Thus, they are also called Wet Blue—in contrast to the Wet White, which is created during tawing and especially during tanning fur. Here, non-dyeing synthetic tanning agents and aluminum salts

Tanning upper leather at Hoffmans is still back-breaking work today.

"Vertical hanging" for the hides is a preliminary stage for pit tanning with vegetable bark and fruits.

for, it is put into a milling drum where it is beaten until the desired softness is achieved. The most well-known leather of this type is **nappa leather**. During further work steps, impregnation substances, oil, or wax are applied and badly dyed parts are corrected. Embossing to create **Scotch grain** or **fake crocodile** is also done at this point. During a final ironing process to enhance smoothness and shine even more, especially elegant leather types are created. For leather types produced for use in sports, this work step is omitted.

"feel-good climate" for leather clothing and shoes. Here, the decisive factor is the craftsmanship of the master of dyeing. For drying, the leather hides are first positioned on top of a stretching machine where they are pressed flat and pulled apart, producing a smooth surface. Now the leather hides are put on a heating plate at 104 degrees Fahrenheit [40 degrees Celsius] on which they are smoothed and dried briefly under vacuum in order to fixate the fibers. The actual drying process is done with the hides hanging in drying furnaces.

By slow drying, the leather has time enough to finish the ongoing chemical reactions. Thus, the added tanning and dyeing agents bond even better with the structure of the fibers. Prior to finishing, the leather is tumbled mechanically, then ironed at 190 degrees Fahrenheit [90 degrees Celsius] and pressed smooth again. Now the leather is called "crust."

The first finishing step is to mechanically remove lengthy fibers on the leather's backside with abrasive paper. If the leather is polished on its top side, **nubuck** is created. If an especially soft type of leather is wished

At Rendenbach the bark is still milled by them, as you can see here.

"Scraping machine" at Rendenbach.
By means of the scraping machine, the hides are cleaned on the grain side.
This means they are freed from hair roots and surplus color pigments.

A view of the pit yard of the Rendenbach tannery, the heart of pit tanning.

Chamoising or Chamois Tanning

Chamois leather is tanned by means of blubber or fish oil (usually cod liver oil). The actual tanning is achieved by oxidation of the blubber inside the hides. Chamois leather is pleasantly soft and easy to clean. Usually it is made from sheep, but skins from deer, goats, or cattle are used as well. Chamoising is one of the oldest tanning methods and sometimes is also called **oil tanning**.

Tawing is tanning with aluminum salts, which is the reason it is sometimes also called **alum tanning**. It was replaced almost completely by chrome tanning and nowadays is only used for the tanning of furs and decorative pelts, like hunting trophies. By this tanning method, the leather receives a whitish color hue, which looks very decorative. Tawed leathers have the disadvantage that they are not water-resistant and the tanning substances may be washed off by frequent contact with water. If egg yolk and flour are added to the tanning substances, the result is a so-called glacé tanning or French tawing. Glacé leather is mainly used for gloves and is very sensitive.

The process called **pit tanning, bark tanning,** or **vegetable tanning** is mainly used today for the production of high-quality leather for shoe soles. As one of the best methods worldwide, pit tanning with tanbark from oak has become well established. With this method, no mechanical techniques for speeding up the tanning process are used at all. Moreover, only natural tanning agents, like oak, fir, or mimosa bark, are used, as well as valonia oak and extracts from chestnut and sumac. The basis is formed from bark of young oak and fir trees, because the ratio of tanning agents is highest with them. Oak can be used for all kinds of leather; chestnuts produce a hard type of leather with reddish color, and fir bark creates a lot of acid—therefore, it has to be dosed exactly. Mimosa bark from acacia trees introduces elasticity

This stamp stands for the best quality made in Germany.

and softness to the leather. The cups of the valonia oak, a Mediterranean oak species, contain a very high percentage of tanning substances of up to thirty-two percent, which provide stiffness and toughness to the leather. Besides the tanning substances used, time is also of essential importance. The longer the hides are exposed to the tanbark (tanning substances, especially bark), the deeper the tanning substances penetrate into the skin.

The actual tanning process consists of three steps. During the first step, the cleaned and de-haired skins are hung into a pit measuring six by six feet [two by two meters] and is six feet [two meters] deep. This step can consist of up to sixteen of these pits in which the skins are exposed to increasing concentrations of tanning liquid. This way, over tanning, which occurs when the skins are immersed immediately in a fresh tanning liquid, is avoided. Because the big particles of the tanning agent immediately bond with the skins, they block the way for the smaller ones and thus prevent the leather from becoming thoroughly tanned. The entire process needs about four weeks to completion. During the next step, the skins are put into another pit. This pit is filled about halfway with an even more strongly concentrated tanning liquid. The skins are put on top of a grid horizontally, with a layer of crushed tanbark between each of them, and then lowered into the pit. There they stay for about twelve weeks. Sometimes, they are put into a new pit with fresh tanning liquid after six weeks. The last step is the lay away. Now the actual oak bark pit tanning takes place. The skins are put into a pit whose bottom is thickly covered with tanbark. A layer of tanbark is also put in between each of the skins. After that, weak tan liquor is led into the pit and finally, as an airtight seal, an especially thick layer of tanbark is put on top of everything. In the very end, the pit is weighted down and covered with planks. The skins remain in the lay away pit for nine months. Afterwards, they are cleaned, smoothed, and hung up for drying. To fixate the tanning agents and to achieve great elasticity, the leather is then oiled and compressed with rolls. By this treatment, the leather becomes very resistant to wear and tear. It is not only used for shoe soles, but also for saddles and harnesses. Soft lining leathers and saffian (a.k.a. Morocco or maroquin) as well as sleek leather for processing furniture are produced this way, too.

Finest calf leather in countless colors is produced at the Richard Hoffmans
tannery for customers from around the world.

Leather Types According to Origin

Buffalo leather stems from domesticated Asian water buffaloes. Usually it is dyed with aniline and used as cushion leather, and also, less frequently, for car seats. It is quite resistant to wear, but has the well-known disadvantages of aniline leathers. Buffalo leather has larger pores compared to leather from cattle and the hair canals are clearly visible.

Chevreaux leather is kid leather, which is exclusively chrome-tanned (**chrome-tanned kid**). It is very light, soft, and resistant to wear. Its signature is the crescent-shaped scars as well as its characteristic unstructured wrinkles. **Morocco leather (saffian)** is the name for kid leather bark-tanned with sumac.

Cordovan is special, vegetable-tanned horse leather made from the croups of the animals. Sometimes a special color hue is also called cordovan. Exactly two oval "shells" are received from each horse; thus the name "Shell Cordovan" for the highest quality. The best leather stems mostly from large draft horses. Probably the best shell cordovan is produced in Chicago by the tannery Horween. Exactly one shoe can be made from each of the shells. But since the shells were not conjoined, the fiber structure of the leather is different, which means a pair of shoes results in which different wrinkles are created by walking. Cordovan is especially famous for its extraordinary deep glow and its smooth surface. This makes the leather easy to recognize for amateurs and is also responsible for its perceived value. The shiny surface is created by the treatment of the leather's flesh side, which also provides almost complete water resistance. Shoes from cordovan are extremely comfy because of their elasticity.

Cordovan leather is about ten percent heavier and a bit thicker than calf leather. With the exception of crocodile leather, it is one of the most expensive leather types.

Elkskin leather is very soft, usually chamois-dressed leather. It is used for clothing, shoe uppers, and high-quality bags used in hunting. Elkskin leather is real deer shammy and thus visible mosquito bites and small injuries are seen as certificates for their natural origin.

Elephant leather is pleasantly soft, quite thick, and very wear resistant. But it is hard to get in Germany because many leather dealers and manufacturers shy away from the very stringent import regulations (see the passage about crocodile leather). Elephant leather is especially suited for shoes with robust looks or wear-resistant travel baggage.

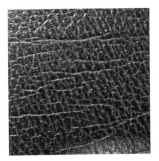

Buffalo leather

Elephant leather

Bison leather

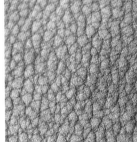

Elkskin leather

Caiman leather

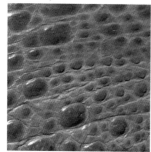

Frog leather

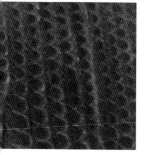

Lizard leather

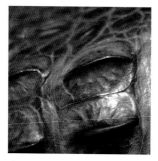

Crocodile leather

Fish leather belongs to the exotic leather types and accordingly is very rare and expensive. Because of its optics, products from fish leather are always very extravagant. Fish leather is very thin (0.5 millimeters) and thus is seldom used by itself. Usually it is used ornamentally and is always backed up by lining leather. The most frequently used fish species are salmon, carp, cod, and trout. Their scales display characteristic patterns. Sharks and rays (see the respective passages) are also used for leather production. Shark leather is usually offered undyed; it has a pronounced roughness and is very resistant to wear.

Frog leather stems from bullfrogs and is soft, flexible, and firm. It is mostly used for small leather products and applications.

Calf leather, especially the high-quality box calf, which stems from calves fed with milk exclusively, is mostly used for exquisite leather products and high-quality shoes. The reason for this is its flexibility accompanied by firmness and toughness. Since one hide is sufficient for most leather products, a uniform fiber structure is the result.

Kangaroo leather is characterized by its high tear resistance, pull resistance, and stability. At the same time, it is thinner and lighter than cow leather. Thus, it is primarily used for sneakers, gloves, and sometimes also for motorcycle apparel.

Crocodile leather actually stems from alligators. It is the most desired reptile leather and the most expensive leather type by far. The reason for this is that, contrary to cow, calf, or lamb, only the skin is used and thus all the costs for raising the animals have to be covered by selling the skins. Nowadays, only skins of bred animals are used, which are all delivered with papers from the organization CITES (Convention on International Trade in Endangered Species of Wild Flora and Fauna), also known as the Washington Convention. Usually skins from young alligators are preferred because they can be treated more easily. Leather with large scales in general is seen as more decorative and thus is desired more than small-scale leather. Crocodile leather per se is very stable and tough. Nevertheless, it is worked very thinly (0.7 mm) because of its low elasticity. Besides that, the leather crackles when bent. Because of this, lining leather is almost always used.

Horse leather—with the exception of cordovan as a special type of leather for shoes—is mostly used for jackets, which are distinguished by high weight and a certain amount of stiffness. Heavily greased, they remind one of U.S. pilot jackets with respect to their shine and their shape, since horse leather is especially favored in the USA.

Horse nappa is very exclusive and comfortable to wear. Since horse nappa is usually ironed aniline leather, the pores stay open, which in turn provides a pronounced patina over time.

Cow leather is especially firm, tough, and relatively thick. It is easy to get and thus reasonably priced. Cow leather with embossed grain is called **Scotch grain**.
This treatment was initially used to cover flaws in the leather. Nowadays, it is only used for decorative purposes and other leather types are used for creating Scotch grain as well.

Sleek leather is vegetable-tanned, moderately greased cow leather. Because of its thickness and toughness, it is primarily used for large, stable leather products such as suitcases, furniture, saddles, and also as sole leather for shoes.

With **velvet sleek leather** the grain has been slightly buffed. **Vachette leather** (French: vache = cow) is thin, greased, and sleek cow leather, which is produced by splitting. Usually it is vegetable-tanned and used for furniture. Rarely can you find chrome-tanned split leather, which is mainly used as car leather.
A specialty is **thick bull leather**, the highest quality of which has a thickness of about 4 millimeters. Unfortunately, you can by no means call it modestly priced.

Russian leather is a leather type made from young cows or calves, usually vegetable-

Deer leather

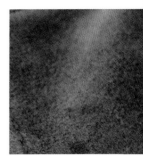

Deer leather, chamois-dressed

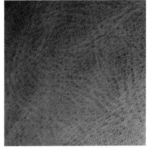

Wapiti, fat-tanned

Calf leather

Scotch grain

Cordovan

tanned, and has its origins in Russia. Special to it are its treatment with birch tar oil, which provides its hydrophobic quality and the smell of smoke. The quality of insulating against heat and cold turns Russian leather into perfect upper leather for rough-wear shoes, especially shoes for mountain-hiking. But wear-resistant bags and strops for razor blades are also made from Russian leather. Sometimes it is also called **russet upper**.

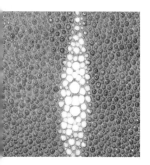

Stingray leather

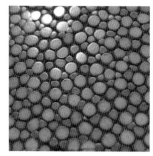

Ground stingray leather

Shark leather

Snake leather

the products made from it. The surface can also be buffed, which smooths the leather and gives it a slightly different appearance.

Sheep leather is almost exclusively used as aniline-treated leather for furniture. Its characteristics are similar to those of kid leather, but the quality varies. Thus, lamb leather is used for clothing, bags, and leather accessories. Lamb leather is often embossed and, especially for clothing, is often worked into lamb nappa.

Snake leather is mainly produced from the skins of pythons and boas, but skins of other snake species are partly used as well. As is the case with almost all reptile leathers, thin snake leather (about 0.5 mm) is not very elastic either and thus is always strengthened by lining leather. Exotic and eye-catching, it is well-liked for fashion accents.

Pig leather from domesticated pigs is mainly used as moderately priced leather for clothing and as lining leather for shoes and bags. Suitcases and briefcases are also made from pig leather. Pig leather has a lower tear resistance than other leather types and consequently is not used for protective gear.

Peccary is leather from wild new world pigs living in South America. As a type of leather made from wild mammals, peccary has more scars than the leather of domesticated animals. It is very flexible and is mainly used for small, soft leather products and gloves.

Lavalina leather is aniline cow leather that was treated to become water-repellent. It has the typical disadvantages of aniline, such as susceptibility to stains and a tendency for colors to fade. A couple of years ago, it was especially common in the area of leather furniture. Pigmented Lavalina leather is used nowadays in automobiles.

Stingray leather is leather made from stingray. It belongs to the fish leathers and thus to the exotic leathers. The hemispherical structure of its surface reminds one of pearls and is unique among leathers. In addition, there is a white, rhombic area on the back. Thus, stingray leather is a very eye-catching, decorative material with the hard surface of the pearls contributing to the toughness of

Ostrich leather is a very exclusive and eye-catching leather type. It contains lots of fibers and sewing parts together is quite difficult. Characteristic are the "goose bumps" on its surface, from which the feathers originally grew. Because of these pimples, ostrich leather has a very extravagant look. Shoes, straps for wrist watches, and other small leather products are made from this leather.

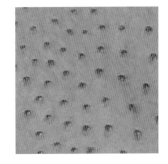 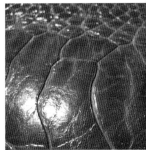

Ostrich leather   Leather from an ostrich's leg

Leather Types According to Dyeing Processes

Aniline leather is a type of leather with open pores and without surface pigmentation, which is treated with soluble dyes. The natural scars stay intact this way, which is why only flawless hides are used for the production of aniline leather. Otherwise, mosquito bites or injuries would still be visible on the finished leather. Thus aniline leather is usually more expensive than leather of the same origin, which has been dyed on its surface. In case a slight pigmentation has been applied to the grain (surface), which covers the pores partly, the term **semi-aniline leather** is used. If the pores are covered completely, we are dealing with **pigmented leather**. Pigmented leather is also called **surface-dyed** or **one-sided dyed** leather. It feels smoother and cooler than aniline or semi-aniline leather. If you don't know which leather type you have, the water test will be helpful. If the water droplet is absorbed quickly, the leather in question is aniline leather. If the droplet is absorbed slowly, it's semi-aniline leather. And if the droplet isn't absorbed at all, the leather is pigmented. But you had better be careful and choose an inconspicuous spot for testing. One drop of water can be enough to create a stain on aniline or semi-aniline leather, which can't be removed. Despite its fluffy surface, aniline leather belongs to the smooth leather types.

Ostrich leather shoes for actor Ralf Möller.

Bentley leather seats are made from vegetable-tanned cow leather in traditional, British manual work. Bentley produces the best car leather seats available.

Leather Types According to Surface Consistency

Antique leathers are mainly used for the production of furniture, especially Chesterfield furniture, backpacks, and hunting bags. Antique leathers possess a light basic color. A second, darker color is added by wiping, then rubbed off again. Thus, this kind of leather is sometimes also called **rub-off leather**. Usually the leather used is cow nappa.

Greased leather is the general term for leather types whose surface has been treated with a fat-containing glaze. This way, they quickly receive some patina, which in turn makes this leather type interesting for furniture, but also bags and shoes. If nubuck is provided with such a layer of fat, it is called **pull-up leather**.

The surface treatment of leather is called *dressing*. Usually it consists of *grounding, pigment coating,* and *top coat,* also called *finish*. The leather is grounded with aniline colors. This way not only the pores are already filled, but the pigmentation will also adhere better. Finally, clear varnish is added and thus the leather is sealed in order to achieve optimal water resistance.

Patent leather is mainly used for festive shoes, elegant lady's handbags, and fetishes. Usually cow or calf leather is used in the production of patent leather. A varnish is applied to the surface in several thick layers, which creates the unique gloss. Patent leather is very susceptible to temperature and thus hardly suited for everyday products. Patent leather belongs to the leather types with coating.

This should not be confused with **PU-leather**, which is also used in the production of furniture. The PU stands for polyurethane, with which these leathers are coated. PU-leather is cheap polyurethane-coated split leather, which is made to look like grain leather but is of inferior quality. PU-leather is also called **bycast leather**.

Friction-glazed leather is leather with a surface that receives a high gloss by pressure and frictional heat on its surface. By the movements during this process, the pores are partially closed, which causes the high gloss. Especially decorative are friction-glazed horse and reptile leather. Unfortunately, this kind of enhancement is very sensitive. The gloss can be damaged by intense contact with water.

Smooth leather refers to all types of leather that were treated with the grain (the side with the hair) on the outside.

Coarse leather is used for leather types that are buffed on the grain or flesh side and thus receive a fibrous surface structure. Sometimes coarse leather is also called **shammy leather**. This isn't correct, because real shammy leather is only made from wild animals like deer, chamois, moose, and others. Smooth leather from slightly buffed grain split turns into coarse leather and then is called **nubuck**. Strongly buffed leather from the flesh split is named **velour leather**, also called velour split. In case the whole skin is used for the production and it is strongly buffed on its backside, high-quality velour is created. Since nubuck is made from the thicker, more stable upper split, it is usually of higher quality than velour. This is buffed more strongly, which creates longer fibers. In general, all coarse leathers are soft to the

Velour leather

Nubuck leather

touch and have an almost fluffy surface, which unfortunately becomes greasy over time.

Nappa leather is the term for full-grain smooth leather that didn't receive any correction of its surface (e.g. by means of embossing) and which—in contrast to traditional leather types such as calf leather—has usually been softened by means of milling (see chapter on tanning). It is always the soft alternative, such as calf nappa. But a distinction according to purpose is also possible, e.g., furniture nappa or glove nappa. Nappa leather can be treated aniline, semi-aniline, or pigmented, and it is almost always thoroughly dyed. This is a special feature of nappa leather. The type of treatment can also influence the designation of the leather, e.g., semi-aniline horse nappa. Nappa leather is mainly used for clothing and furniture. The expression "embossed nappa," which sometimes can be found, is total nonsense, because embossing per se is a correction of the surface structure.

Full grain leather is a type of leather whose grain side is completely intact and which wasn't manipulated with respect to thickness and surface consistency.

History of Shoe and Leather Care

Collonil delivery truck and employees around 1920.

Prior to the invention of shoe polish by chemist Philipp Adam Schneider, associate of wax wares manufactory Werner & Mertz in Mainz, Germany, in 1901, "shoe cream" had been used over the course of centuries. Modern leather care, too, only developed based on the shoe care products of the last 110 years. Since shoes are the leather products that are most stressed, efforts to maintain shoes have been exceptionally high throughout time. Leather clothes and especially saddles were cared for by means of wax rods, which were not satisfying with respect to their use and results. One recipe for shoe cream used prior to 1900 reads as follows: "Take sulfur, soot, syrup, and molasses; stir all of it with water until you get a viscous mush and then fill this, when it is already partly dry, into a chip-wood box."

Kiwi advertisement poster around 1920.

Bottling at Collonil around 1920.

Collonil advertisement poster around 1950.

From the very beginning, the manufacturers of care products paid attention to the image of their brands.

Sometimes bone charcoal (spodium) was used instead of soot. The protective effects of this mixture were bad to non-existent, and the created gloss was mediocre at best. In addition, this shoe cream was not water-resistant and lost color as well. During dry weather this meant that either the legs or the trousers got dirty; during rainy weather the spot where the shoes were left after being outdoors was stained as well. Besides that, the shoe cream was unusable for the colored leather shoes that came into vogue toward the end of the nineteenth century. For these shoes saponified carnauba wax and also bees wax was available from 1881 onward, but these didn't create any shine. For this purpose, American leather varnishes were available, which were based on spirit, turpentine oil, or dissolved shellac wax. They had to be applied with a brush and had a high gloss. In turn, they had no effect with respect to care and ruined the leather optics in the long run,

The war was a real blessing for many manufacturers.

because the entire leather was smeared with varnish, which clogged up the pores.

Only Philipp Adam Schneider combined both methods, which was seen as a jump start for an entirely new economic branch. On September 28, 1901, the patent office of Berlin documented the entry of the brand name "Erdal." The name was derived from the former address of the company, Erthalstrasse 5, which in turn was named after elector and archbishop of Mainz, Friedrich Karl Joseph von Erthal. In the Palatine dialect "Erthal" sounds like "airdaal," which in written German became "Erdal." Today 9,000 cans of Erdal shoe polish are produced every hour, partially for other brands as well.

In 1919, the company Eg-Gü of Dresden, Germany, filled shoe-polish into tubes for the first time worldwide. This was not only a big success for Eg-Gü, but a boom for the whole industry of care products, which quickly copied this way of packaging. This allowed the new shoe polish to be carried on trips easily and without the risk of leaking.

Die letzten Vorbereitungen wurden getroffen. Behandlung der Skistiefel mit „TIEROWA" in Srinagar (Indien)

Many of the brand names for shoe polish that existed then, such as Nigrin, Kavalier, Lodix, Agal, and Heka, are no longer available. Either they cancelled the production of leather care products, they were taken over, or they don't exist anymore.

Since the 1970s, fewer and fewer leather care products are bought. In Germany, which has almost eighty-two million inhabitants, only about 65 million dollars [fifty million euros] were spent on leather care products in 2010. Discounting children and adolescents, every adult person spends about a dollar thirty [one euro] per year on leather care. Here, each euro is well-invested money, all the more if high-quality care products are bought, which always ought to be done. All leather products repay you for their purchase in the long run with prolonged durability, better functionality, and better appearance.

During the first ascent of the Nanga Parbat in the Himalayas, the mountain
climbers rely on Collonil leather oil to keep their shoes watertight.

All Manufacturers
at a Glance

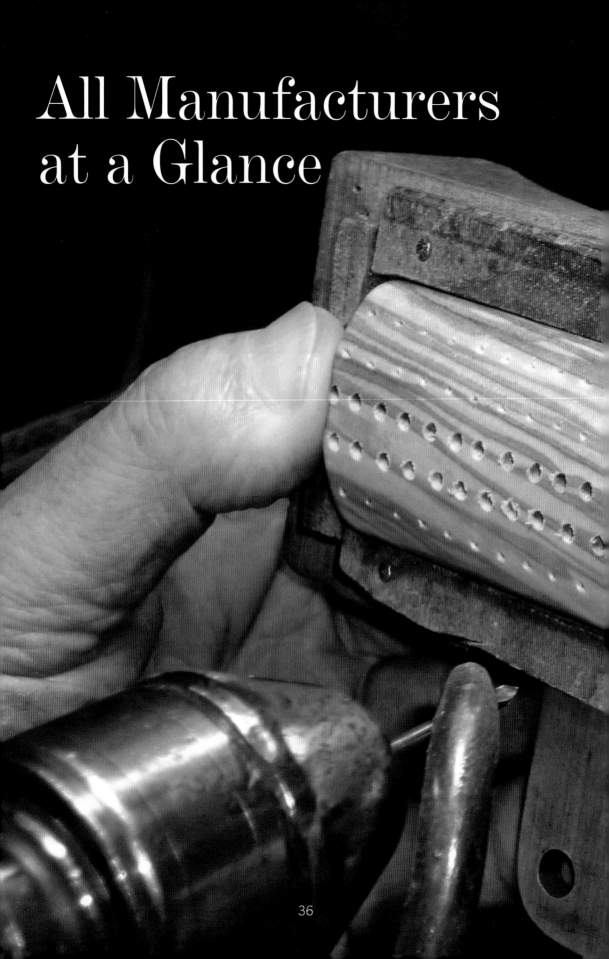

Abbeyhorn

The horn polishing company of the family Humpherson, in the English town Bewdley, was founded in 1749 and belonged to the Humphersons for 171 years. In 1912, the company moved to Gloucester; in 1920, the company was sold to Mr. Grove. He was a relative of the Groves from Halesowen, England, who are famous for the production of horn buttons, which can be traced back to the sixteenth century. The company was sold to Percy Leresche in 1923, after only three years. Inspired by signposts in Llanthony Road showing the direction to the ancient "Llanthony Abbey," Mr. Leresche renamed the manufactory "The Abbey Horn Works." In 1932, Mr. Leresche moved the company to Kendal in Cumbria. There it was merged with the old horn comb manufactory "James Troughton & Sons;" Jim Troughton became a partner. In 1955, the company was sold to Mr. and Mrs. John Barnes. Percy Leresche still worked together with John Barnes until his death a few years later. During this time, exports boomed

and the manufactory is renamed to "Abbey Horn of Kendal Ltd." In 1980, Paul Cleasby entered the company as an apprentice for grinding and polishing horn. After working for the company for eleven years, he bought it in 1991. Paul Cleasby moved the manufactory a few miles to an old eighteenth century mill in the village of Holme. The company's name was changed to "Abbeyhorn of Lakeland." The Scottish horn polishing company "Horncraft," from Irvine in the southwestern county Ayrshire, was bought by the Cleasby family and the name of the entire company was changed to "Abbeyhorn." Besides spoons, traditional Scotish goods, and jewelry, the company produces especially high-quality and nicely-shaped shoehorns from West African Zebu horns, sometimes in combination with handles from stag antlers. All horn products stem from Scottish red deer, West African zebu cattle, Indian water buffalo or British domesticated sheep. They make quality shoehorns. www.abbeyhorn.co.uk

Alvoro

Alvoro was founded in 1999 by the designers Alvo von Römer and Rudolf Spangenberg. The company's name was derived from the first names of both founders, Alvo and Rolf. The founding of the company was based on a realization that while high-quality handmade and custom shoes existed, no suitable corresponding product with respect to furniture for shoes and shoe care products existed that would provide the possibility for individual shoe care in the cultivated ambiance of one's own apartment. Thus, the declared goal of the company was to create special pieces of furniture to be integrated into the home's surroundings.

They introduced their program of products with boxes for shoe care made from solid wood and leather. The customer can choose between two variants with respect to the internal layout. Because of their compact size, the shoe care boxes are easy to carry and stow away. For the top of the line products, the company created the bigger and more elaborately produced shoe care chests. Similar to the boxes, you can choose from woods like maple, mahogany, cherry, beech, nut, rosewood, or burl wood. For the fittings, you can choose from steel, brass, or leather. In general, every special wish of the customer is taken into account, if at all possible. The shoe rest, which is mounted on top of each chest and allows shoe care while wearing the shoes, can be removed and then used as a bootjack. Boxes as well as chests can be ordered already filled.

The most recent development is modular shoe boxes for stowing made from maple, nut, or MDF (medium-density fiberboard). On the front and back sides they have openings for ventilation and better drying; inside they have a moveable grid, which makes it easier to put shoes in and take them out of the box. The boxes can be augmented by a box with shoe care products of the same looks and finish. The surfaces are available with a natural, waxed, or lacquered finish. The shoe boxes as well as the chests are intricately made by hand in Germany.
www.alvoro-design.de

Bama

In 1914, Curt Baumann bought a sewing machine and a manual die cutter in Dresden, Germany, for 750 Reichsmark and started with the production of insoles. The company was very successful and by 1939, 400 assistants were already employed. After the Second World War, in 1945, the production was in Mosbach. In 1949, the newly erected manufactory had to expand again. In the following decade, the first foreign subsidiaries were established. But very soon afterwards, the capacity for production was once again too small. Thus, in 1965 a second plant was built in Mosbach. In 1980, Bama became the clear market leader in Germany. In 1993 the company expanded to Poland due to cost reasons and a new factory was erected there. Thus the work, which is very labor-intensive, could be continued economically. The U.S. trust Sara Lee took over Bama in 1997 and integrated the company into its European branch of shoe care products. In addition, the entire European production of Sara Lee's shoe care products was concentrated at the Polish facility of Bama and only the administration stayed at Mosbach. In 2011, Bama, like the shoe care brand Kiwi, which also belonged to the Sara Lee trust, was sold to the U.S. enterprise S.C. Johnson. Besides the classical

insoles and other furnishings, Bama also offers a wide variety of shoe care products. Emulsion creams in pots and tubes can be found in the assortment as well as outdoor wax cream, leather grease, cleaning foam and lotions for care. The disinfection spray is especially well-approved by shoe care services in premium hotels.
www.bama-tana.com

Bama has a great selection of sprays and cleaners.

Bense & Eicke

Bense & Eicke was founded as a tannery by merchant Bense and pharmacist Eicke in Einbeck, Lower Saxony, Germany, in 1887. The main bulk of the sales volume was achieved by auxiliary products for tanneries and leather factories worldwide. After a conflagration, the company was rebuilt in the new industrial area of Einbeck in 1905. Aside from products for horse care, which are still produced under the brand name Parisol today, the company already produced the first leather care products and leather dyes back then.

In 1936, the company Bense & Eicke was purchased by Walter Schmidt from Hannover and belonged to his company network. On January 10, 1958, Albert Reinecke, now limited partner of the company, acquired Bense & Eicke. At this time, among other products, special dyes for coating leather were manufactured there, especially for soccer balls, which were also procured by Adidas and Puma.

In 1986, another fire destroyed the company's entire production plant. Production was up and running again in Einbeck's district Edemissen within four weeks after the fire. In the following years, the existing buildings were augmented by two modern facilities for production and storage that have changed according to present-day needs. In 1989, the company was converted into a limited partnership. The learned chemist Dietmar Reinecke, son of Albert Reinecke, was chosen as an associate. Today, with Christoph Reinecke as CEO, the third generation is already at the helm.

Under the brand name B & E, Bense & Eicke offers leather fat and oils, which are mainly based on bees wax, petrolatum, lanolin, perfume, jojoba oil, and neat's-foot oil.

Besides their use for leather clothes, they are also very well suited for use with saddles and harnesses, because Bense & Eicke has much experience in this area. Shoe polish is offered under the name Walin, and leather blacking is branded Tiger. The superb and prize-winning saddle soap should not go unmentioned either. Bense & Eicke does not use any silicone or silicone oil in their products, because it limits the ability of the leather to breathe. www.bense-eicke.de

The saddle soap in the resealable can is easy to apply.

BNS

The BNS—Bergal, Nico & Solitaire Vertriebs GmbH—was founded in Mainz, Germany, in 1999 and focuses on the distribution of shoe care products, insoles, footbeds, shoe trees, and shoestrings to specialized shoe dealers, shopping malls, wholesale traders, and to orthopedic shoemakers as well. The company's ownership is divided equally between the manufacturer of shoe trees, Nico Norbert Schmid GmbH & Co. KG, and the company Werner & Metz GmbH.

The company's headquarters are located at Mainz; the main production areas are in Germany, Austria, and Poland. BNS stands for products and services of high quality and provides the customer with positive feedback. Not least because of this, the company has become a market leader in this area of expertise after only twelve years of existence. However, the three brands that comprise the name have existed much longer than the BNS itself, which is almost unknown to consumers.

The company Nico was founded in 1959 and initially focused on the production of shoe trees made from plastics, which were modern at that time. Meanwhile, Nico leads the world market for all types of shoe trees from its headquarters at Fellbach (close to Stuttgart), Germany.

The brand Bergal was created at the beginning of the twentieth century by a certain Mr. Bergmann, who gave part of his name to create the designation for the brand. From the very beginning, the trade focused on shoestrings. After the Second World War, the company's future path was twofold; in the Federal Republic of Germany, the brand name Bergal was revived by its owners at Wuppertal, while the production plant at Erfurt was nationalized and controlled by the GDR regime (Bergal Erfurter Flechtwerke), though keeping the brand name Bergal. Other braided products, such as wicks and wire insulations were also produced for the GDR's

national economy. In West Germany, the range of products was broadened by insoles. After the reunion of Germany in 1989, the production plant at Erfurt became part of the business structure once more. Today, Bergal insoles and footbeds are manufactured in a joint venture of BNS. The shoe strings are still produced at Erfurt.

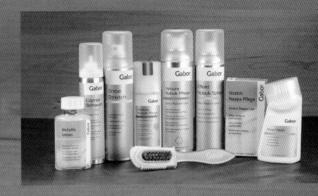

The brand Gabor is completely made by BNS.

Products made by Solitaire, initially founded in Berlin as the subsidiary of a British business, were already sold by specialized shoe dealers and shoemakers from 1927 onward. In 1929, Werner & Mertz at Mainz, Germany, purchased all shares of the company and the brand name. Until the end of the 1960s, Solitaire—still written Solitär at that time—was *the* brand of shoemakers and small shoe dealers with a broad base for distribution in Germany. The rapid concentration process among shoemakers at the beginning of the 1970s and the increasing concentration among shoe dealers changed the situation in this sector effectively, which means that Solitaire nowadays can be found mainly at specialized shoe dealers and big chain stores. Today, only shoe care products are distributed under the brand name Solitaire.

In 1996, the brand Shoeboy's was introduced. At first, only containers with one type of polish were available in six different colors. Two years later, the assortment was augmented by a few more articles and since then broadened into a full product line encompassing shoe care, insoles, shoestrings, and shoe trees. Now Shoeboy's is even asked for in foreign countries.

In addition, the brands Búfalo and Morello are also produced and distributed by BNS. While Búfalo, like Shoeboy's, offers a full product line with respect to shoe furnishings, the brand Moreno only offers leather dyes and special products for shoemakers, which are somewhat more complicated in use but nevertheless very effective.

BNS also created many brands for shoe trade chains and also produces the Gabor line of shoe care products under license.

The German Olympic teams also trust in BNS as a supplier. For many years, German athletes have traveled to the Olympic Games equipped with shoe trees of the brand Nico. Meanwhile, the Olympic athletes receive in addition the complete shoe care equipment from BNS, which was rewarded with the title official supplier of the German Olympic team with respect to auxiliary equipment for shoes. www.bns-mainz.com

Shoeboy's is also a BNS brand.

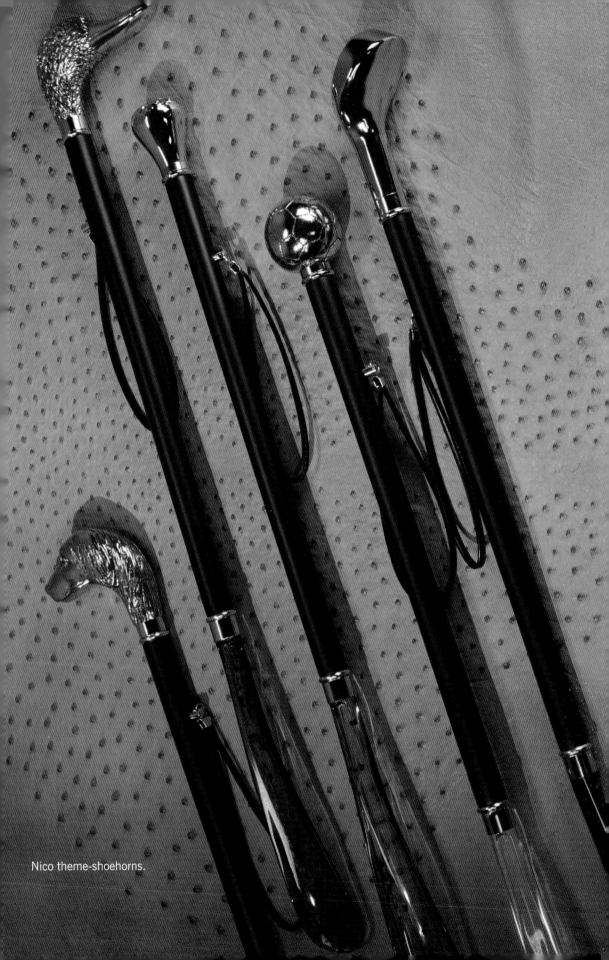

Nico theme-shoehorns.

Burgol

In 1921, the family Grüttner of Burgdorf, Switzerland, started the production of shoe polish. The name Burgol is derived from the town's name Burgdorf. At first, sales were exclusively done in the area of Emmental. Back then, the shoe polish was already filled into the characteristic tin cans. Son-in-law Alfred Jährmann took over in 1945 and moved the production to Aarwangen. The castle of Aarwangen is the company emblem, which still decorates all Burgol cans today. The mixtures were melted in large cooking pans and then decanted. Slowly the number of customers rose who were living in the canton of Bern and were supplied by means of bicycles until the 1950s. In collaboration with a laboratory, Alfred Jährmann refined the mixtures and thus recipes were created that are still in use today. Because a successor was lacking, Jährmann sold the company in 1983 to Siegenthaler AG, which has been producing and selling the palm wax shoe polish since then. Great emphasis is put on the manual production and the use of natural resources such as carnauba wax, bees wax, essential turpentine oil, and natural dyes. Burgol shoe polish is offered in twelve color hues and as sport wax for rough-wear leather. www.burgol.de

Centralin

In 1897, the families Kircher and Schmachtenberg founded the company Schmachtenberg & Kirchner in Northrhine-Westfalia as a trading company for shoe furnishings. Later, in 1906, the Centralin corporation was founded, which has been in the possession of the Kircher family ever since. The name Centralin was derived from the center of a target. Since especially hunters took care of their boots, even in ancient times, present-day hunters should get the impression that they can always hit the mark with the shoe care products of Centralin. Even prior to 1906, products for the care of furniture were added. Candles were also added to the product line and distributed until 1955. Today Centralin, as a medium-sized company, produces and distributes established products for the care of furniture, floors, and shoes. In addition to this broad assortment, Centralin has a leading market position in Germany with respect to gas and lighter fluid for cigarette lighters. In 2003, the aerosol works in Herne were integrated into the company and thus the leadership was further expanded. Based on the high technical competence of the affiliate in bottling aerosol sprays, creams, and fluids for body hygiene, hair sprays, insect sprays, and air deodorizers, many new products were added, which partly were also fillings for other brands. Centralin especially emphasizes a good cost-performance ratio of its products and high environmental sustainability. Thus, Centralin prefers biodegradable ingredients for its products. Because it lacked solvents, the cream in tubes was the first product that received the so-called PROOF-seal by the TÜV Rheinland in the November 2010 issue of the German magazine Ökotest, which tested twelve different types of shoe polish sold in tubes. Centralin was the winner of the test, with the mark "good." With respect to hard wax pastes, Centralin achieved second best. In addition to the wide assortment of shoe polish in tubes and cans, aerosol sprays for impregnation, leather grease, fluid leather care products, and tubes with sponges for application, a wide array of brushes for shoe care is also on offer.
www.centralin.com

Collonil

In 1909, Karl Esslen founded his one-man service in Berlin, Germany. His first product was the tough leather oil Collan Olja from the Swedish manufacturer Olsen, for which Karl Esslen was rewarded the contract for importation into Germany. Pretty soon he needed help and hired the brothers Paul and Walter Salzenbrodt, who quickly advanced to managers of the small company. Although the first large order was made by a company producing drive belts, the ropy oil quickly established itself in the shoe industry because of its good qualities with respect to care and protection against moisture. Due to its great success, space at the plant was already running out in 1912. The beginning of World War I, of course, limited corporate ambitions; the brothers Salzenbrodt were recruited into the army. Karl Esslen, whose parents had adopted citizenship of Luxembourg, was able to continue work and the increased need for water-repelling materials for soldiers' boots was benefitting sales volume. Even Count Zeppelin used Collonil leather oil for waterproofing the mooring ropes of the airships named after him. In a letter to Karl Essen he confirmed "the proven qualities" of the oil. After the return of the Salzenbrodt brothers at the end of the war in 1918, the company did business under the name Esslen

& Co. GmbH and the founders decided to expand their one-product-company, developing high quality shoe care products under the name Collonil.

The name Collonil, referencing the viscous, sticky leather oil, is derived from the French "coller," which means "to glue." Karl Esslen bought the raw materials, since he—as a citizen of Luxembourg—wasn't bound by the limitations of the Treaty of Versailles and had good international connections. Paul Salzenbrodt was responsible for the technical sector and his brother Walter for the commercial realm. Early success was achieved in the areas of care for patent leather and coarse leather. In 1921 the company expanded once again and moved to Mühlenbeck, a suburb of Berlin. With the freshly introduced "Glanz-Fett," shoes for the first time could be made water-repellent, as well as glossy. This product nowadays is available with improved composition under the name "Anti-Rain Wetterputz."

Karl Esslen died in 1929. But the success nevertheless continued in 1930, when a subsidiary was opened in Austria. In the years following, Collonil also began manufacturing care products for leather clothing. In 1935, Paul Salzenbrodt died. With the beginning of World War II, production at Collonil slowed down. Expropriation followed the end of the war and Walter Salzenbrodt fled to West Berlin, where he dared to start from scratch again in 1948 without the help of Karl Esslen's widow. Thus the Walter Salzenbrodt & Co. GmbH was created. With the start of the economic miracle, people became interested in fashion again and thus the demand for leather and shoe care products rose as well. Collonil care products for coarse leather were offered in a variety of hues. In the 1950s the products were exported to France, Denmark, and the Netherlands and Collonil—as the first company worldwide—introduced tubes with a sponge for application to the market.

In 1952, Walter Salzenbrodt's son Rolf and his cousin Hans took over management of the company, which was now called Salzenbrodt & Co. KG. Shortly thereafter, the company moved once more, this time to Berlin-Wittenau, where the company is still located today. In 1962, a Himalaya-expedition reached the Nanga Parbat with the help of Collonil "Sport Wax." The first aerosol spray was developed around the same time. In 1985, Rolf Salzenbrodt retired and his son Michael took over. In 1986, Hans Salzenbrodt died and proxy holder Gert Thuner moved up into management until the time he started to receive retirement pay. Michael Salzenbrodt died in 1997 and in 1998 the company was freshly organized under the leadership of the new CEO Frank Becker. Australia, Taiwan, and the Middle East were made accessible as new markets for export, as were the countries of the former Eastern Bloc. Especially Russia, with its still flourishing fur industry for which Collonil produces care products as well, has risen to become the largest exportation market. In the first decade of the new millennium, new product lines were introduced for car leather. A new product line based on nanotechnology and a new premium line called "Collonil 1909" were introduced as well.

www.collonil.de

Colonia Shoe and Leather Care

In 2010, the sisters Nicola and Kim Himer together developed a series of leather care products of their own, which has been available under the brand name Colonia Shoe and Leather Care since 2011. *Colonia* is the Latin term for "the younger." Since Colonia Shoe and Leather Care at the time of its foundation was the youngest brand for leather care and, moreover, is located at Cologne, the choice of the brand name Colonia Shoe and Leather Care suggested itself. Colonia leather care products are available as washing cream, emulsion cream, leather grease, dye for the rim of soles, detergents, conditioners, oil and aerosol sprays; brushes and shoe trees are also available. For real individualists, Colonia offers handmade shoehorns from horns chosen by the customers themselves. Another specialty is shoe polish fitted especially to the customer's shoe leather and prepared from a mixture of beeswax, carnauba wax, classy dye pigments, and a variety of oils. The cans for care products can also be individualized and printed with the customer's name. Handmade leather care travel sets from various leather types are made according to the customer's wishes at Colonia by Kim and Nicola Himer. www.colonia-shoecare.com

Brushes and shoe trees are also part of the Colonia program.

The star chef Johann Lafer showed enthusiasm about the fact that shoe cream can also be cooked.

Dunkelman & Son— Dasco

Freddie Dunkelman was born in West Ham, a quarter of London, but grew up in Canada until he was seventeen. There he discovered his passion for hockey. After his return to England in 1937, he earned his name as a hockey player and as such was a member of the Olympic team in 1948. Already in June 1946, he founded the company Dunkelman & Son, nowadays better known as Dasco. In a small workshop in London's Battersea district, he started with the production of hockey sticks and skates. Although the business with the hockey equipment went well and Dunkelman exported his goods to Canada and Europe, he searched for a possibility to bridge the gap during the summer months. In 1950, Freddie Dunkelman by chance met Georg Hartmann, whose company produced wooden shoe trees in Germany, and thus Dunkelman was appointed sales representative for Great Britain. A year later, the shoe trees were already a great success. At the same time the production of wooden inlays for bootlegs was started and the company also joined in the business of selling shoe polish. In 1957, a manufacturer of plastic shoe trees was bought up. When hockey became less and less popular, sales of sports articles were stopped, and by the end of the fifties the change to shoe care products as the core business of the company was complete. At this point, the upmarket specialized stores in London were already provided with shoe trees made from wood and plastics. In the sixties, bootstrap stretchers were added. In 1965, Freddie Dunkelman moved the company to Desborough, Northamptonshire, where it is still located. There he built a new plant and storehouse. In 1967, shoe last manufacturer Foster Brothers, also located at Desborough, was bought up. The bootstrap stretchers introduced in 1968 for the knee-high ladies'

Dasco shoe trees made of varnished beech tree.

boots, which were in vogue at the time, evolved into a worldwide success. About the same time, the brand name Dasco became a registered trademark and from then on it appeared on all of Dunkelman's articles. In the seventies, wooden sandals and clogs were produced and by the end of the '70s inlays and shoestrings were added. Later on, aerosol sprays and shoe polish with integrated sponge for application were added. Recent products include gel-based inlays. In 1997, Freddie Dunkelman gave up his management position, but stayed in the company until 2007. He died in 2010.

The company is still in family possession and is now led by the siblings Stephen and Jon Dunkelman, Jane Woodnutt, and the chairman of the management board, Philip Luckett. Today Dunkelman & Sons is Great Britain's leading manufacturer of shoe furnishings. Besides shoe trees and bootstrap stretchers, shoe polish, shoestrings, inlays, and shoehorns, the assortment of Dasco also includes articles that are hard to find, such as shoe wideners. Dasco products nowadays are available in forty-three countries and are also produced and packaged for other companies. To the illustrious circle of customers belong companies with impressive-sounding names such as Crockett & Jones, Church Shoes, John Lobb, Harrods, Russell & Bromley, Hugo Boss, Prada, and others.
www.dunkelman.com

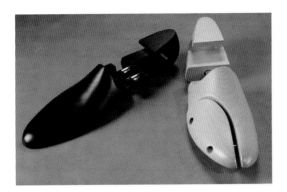

The Hey care series is a brand of Effax.

Dasco shoe tree with handle for easy removal.

Eduard Meier

Peter Eduard Meier and his sister Brigitte now, as the thirteenth generation, lead the company founded by Hans Maier that was first mentioned in 1596 as the shoe trading house of Eduard Maier in Munich, Germany. High-ranking noblemen, such as the kings of Saxony and the sovereigns of Hohenzollern-Sigmaringen, were among the customers of the house. In 1895, Eduard Meier became supplier of the Bavarian royal court. Brigitte and Peter Meier, as well as their team, are real "shoe whisperers." Today they surely head one of Germany's best shoe stores. Peter Meier developed his own Eduard Meier shoe care product line, which meets the highest requirements. In addition, as one of the first persons to do so, he already offered shoe care seminars of very high standards to his customers in the 1980s.

Today, interested persons learn everything worth knowing about shoe care in a seminar taking several hours. Besides the large assortment of welt-sewn, ready-made shoes for ladies and gentlemen and the possibility to order custom made shoes, Eduard Meier nowadays also offers high-quality clothing and equipment from leather, loden, and tweed for hunting and the outdoors. A large choice among high-quality shoe care products has existed for several decades. Eduard Meier offers its own hard wax pastes, emulsion creams, leather detergents, and oil based care products. The best shoe trees, shoehorns, and polishing brushes, as well as brushes to provide a shiny appearance, are on offer, too. Besides the shoe care seminars, Eduard Meier also has a DVD teaching how to care for shoes and a reading primer on shoe care among the goods in its sales catalog.
www.edmeier.de

Effax

The *Chemische Industriegesellschaft* mbH Mannheim (Chemical Industrial Corporation at Mannheim, Germany) was founded on January 18, 1906, and from the very beginning produced means for shoe care under the brand name *"Effax Schuh und Lederpflege"* [Effax Shoe and Leather Care]. Another supporting leg was products for horse care, such as healing ointments and ointments for hoofs under the brand name Effol. From July 10, 1909, onwards, the company group did business as *Chemische Fabrik Effax August Spoerl & Co.* GmbH [Chemical Factory Effax August Spoerl & Company]; in 1913 the headquarters moved to Bensheim. In 1936, Herr Schweizer took over the group of companies and thus the name from then on was *Chemische Werke Schweizer & Co.* GmbH [Chemical Plants Schweizer & Company]. Since 1997, the Schweizer-Effax GmbH belongs to the Eimermacher group located in Nordwalde. Leather and horse care are still an inherent part of the assortment, which over the last few decades was extended to include textile and domestic care products.

Today, a staff of nineteen produces a large assortment of leather care products in accordance with highest quality standards. Thus only raw materials that are of the same quality as those used in the area of human medicine are used. The entire production is done under the GMP-standard (Good Manufacturing Practice). This standard is an EU-recommendation to assure quality in the manufacturing of medicaments, active substances, food, and forage. Another specialty of all companies within the Eimermacher group is that practically the entire value creation takes place inside the companies. So, besides the production, research, and development, storage, marketing, and distribution are internal and located in Germany. Nowadays, this is self-evident. The constant ecological efforts were rewarded with the eco-profit certificate. This philosophy also convinced the German Olympic Committee for equestrian

The Famaco waxes are well suited for an antique finish.

sport, which chose Effax as its supplier. Today, the leather care program includes leather detergents, leather soap, leather balm, and oil as well as special means for combating mold on leather. It also includes a so-called leather grip stick, an agent that, after application on the

saddle, provides a better grip for the rider. For shoes, clothing, and motorbike outfits, means for waterproofing and several types of leather grease are available. Black leather dye and "leather soft" were developed especially for harnesses, but also have other fields of application.
www.schweizer-effax.com

effax®
Lederöl
Leather Oil • Huile pour cuir • Aceite de cuero
Olio per cuoio • Oleo para couros

effax®
Glycerin-Seife
Glycerine Soap, Savon à la glycérine, Glycerine-zeep, Jabón de glicerina, Glycerinöl

BERGSTEIGER
mit Vaseline   und Lanolin
LEDERFETT

effax®
Leder-Fett
Leather-Grease • effax • Graisse pour cuir • lee
engrasante para cuero • Lederfett

effax
imprägniert   reproofes   imperméabilise
und pflegt   and cares   et soigne

WAX COTTON

Leder

Erdal

On October 23, 1867, the brothers Friedrich Christoph Werner and Georg Werner founded the waxwear factory Gebrüder Werner. In 1878, Georg Mertz joined in and the company's name was changed to Werner & Mertz. Georg Mertz died in 1887 and his brother, the chemist Philipp Adam Schneider, took over his shares and led the company together with Friedrich Christoph Werner. As already told in the chapter History of Shoe and Leather Care (page 30), the company Werner & Mertz, with its brand name Erdal, is seen as the inventor of modern shoe polish. Philipp Adam Schneider was the first to combine wax with solvents and thus created a paste-like cream, which had all the desired qualities for shoe care. The brand name Erdal, which was patented in 1901, was so successful that in 1903 the image of the frog king was added.

The idea behind it was that shoes see the world from the perspective of a frog, that they are "waterproof" and shiny like a frog. And since back then it was customary to decorate oneself with the attributes of noblemen, the frog received a crown. In addition, the first cans had the inscription "in private use at courts." About two decades after the invention of shoe polish, already hundreds of small businesses and a few large companies produced shoe polish themselves. Many had been founded as wax-chandlers, like Werner & Mertz, too. Nowadays, the brand name Erdal only adds a small percentage to the commercial results of the company and Erdal products can instead be found at the supermarket rather than in specialized shops. www.werner-mertz.de

Gregor Chemie filling systems.

Famaco

Famaco was founded as Fama by Frédéric Pfirter in Paris in 1931. On the sixth floor of an apartment house, he first created his shoe polish with the Latin name for "rumor" or "fame." Pfirter took over the logo of a gentleman with top hat from a bottle of port wine he emptied together with a friend while ruminating about marketing for his company. More than two decades later, however, the name had to be changed because it sounded too much like "Lama," a brand name that had already been patented. Thus, the company's name was changed to Famaco.

In 1974, the twenty-four-year-old Alain Pfirter took over his father's firm. With effort, personal commitment, short delivery times, and good service, he led the company to success. Today, hard wax pastes are offered in the most common colors, and creams are offered in a wide variety of color hues. www.famaco-shoecare.de

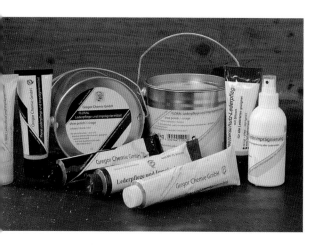

As a little anecdote, it is worth mentioning that this shoe polish applied to the legendary *"Panzerplatten"* ["armor plates"]—hard cookies about one centimeter in thickness that in the German armed forces are used as an emergency food ration—have been and probably still are extremely popular among soldiers for lighting fires of all kinds during bivouacs and tests for recruits.

The leather waterproofing offered as spray can be used on all types of coarse leather. The leather care products comprise a mixture of waxes in solution, oils free from aromatics with an addition of dyes soluble in oil, and hydrophobing agents (silicone oils). The leather waterproofing contains a mixture of aromatic-free oils, emulsifying agents, essential oils, and silicone oil in an aqueous solution. None of the products contains chlorinated hydrocarbons, strong acids, or free alkalis.

www.gregor-chemie.de

Gregor Chemie

Gregor Chemie GmbH was founded by Horst Gregor in 2004. It resulted from buying the bankrupt Floral Chemie GmbH, which was founded in the 1950s, and took over a large part of its product panoply. To this also belonged products for shoe and leather care. Because of their high quality, these products fulfill all requirements with respect to the technical delivery specifications of the German armed forces. Like its predecessor, Gregor Chemie GmbH has been a main supplier of the German armed forces with its leather care products for several decades. The leather care products are also used by other NATO partners. In addition, Gregor Chemie GmbH has a large circle of customers in the areas of forestry, fire departments, the Federal Agency for Technical Relief, as well as in army and outdoor retail sales. The Floral leather care products are especially purchased wherever rough-handled shoes from leather in combination with breathable membranes have to be maintained. While the products dyed in black and brown are meant especially for shoe care, the translucent leather care can also be used for leather clothing and accessories.

Grison—LJW

The French company Grison offers shoe polish, originating from the year 1847 with its roots in Paris. Especially from the 1920s to the 1950s, Grison was well-known in France, Great Britain, and the USA for its good performance.

Today the brand belongs to LJW, a trading company for shoe care products and shoe furnishings. It was founded in 1981 by Lionel John Williams, former CEO of Reckitt & Colman Europa (today Reckitt Benckiser) and is located in Sainte Geneviève des Bois, near Paris. After a strategic reorientation, the company now focuses on its own brands, which, besides Grison, include *Graisse Le Phoque* [The Grease Seal], *Crème Essentielle*, Pedicare, and Recolor. With its shoe and leather care products, Grison covers practically all types of leather. Nevertheless, Grison products are not only meant for shoe care; the company offers care products for leather furniture and leather clothing as well.

Graisse Le Phoque dates back to a Russian businessman of the 1920s who was quite successful with his leather grease based on seal blubber. Since the 1980s the formula hasn't contained any animal products anymore and is solely based on mineral and plant oils.

Crème Essentielle was first marketed in 1983 as a universal cream for all leather colors and for cleaning and maintaining all types of smooth leather. Today it is one of the most important products in the company's portfolio.

Pedicare entered the market in 1996 and offers a wide variety of products with respect to foot care, starting with refreshing creams up to antiperspirant compounds. Recolor offers more than sixty color hues for refreshing the color of or for re-dyeing shoes and other leather products. Products are available for the consumer as well as the professionals. The German company Melvo GmbH from Ludwigsburg took over LJW at the beginning of 2011.
www.ljw.fr

Grison has a large assortment of sprays.

The shoe care program of Grison leaves nothing to be desired.

65

Hölzer Saddle Cabinet Systems

The company Metallbau Hölzer was founded by Erwin Hölzer as a classical plant for processing sheet metal as well as other metal types. The services available range from the simple cutting of sheet metal to the finished product in the areas of store construction, displays, machine covers, and product stands. When Caroline Hölzer, the daughter, started with equestrian sport, it turned out quickly that riding equipment such as saddle, harness, boots, and care products had to be stowed away properly and well protected. They also had to be secured from unauthorized access. Since no satisfying solution existed, the company developed saddle cabinets for stationary storage and movable tournament cabinets for transport to competitions. An integrated safe keeps pilferers from accessing valuables. At the moment, the product line is being expanded to include a special cabinet for polo sports. All cabinets are constructed in various sizes and colors, according to the customer's wishes. Surface structures and the materials used in construction can also be determined by the customer. All cabinets are made in laborious manual work, are very sturdy, and can, of course, be repaired in case of damage.
www.metallbau-hoelzer.de

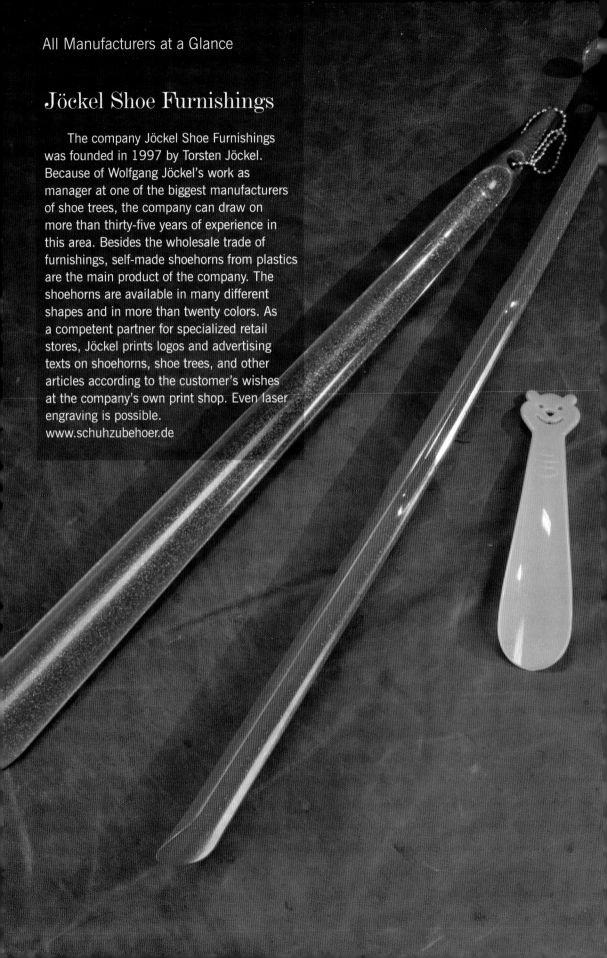

Jöckel Shoe Furnishings

The company Jöckel Shoe Furnishings was founded in 1997 by Torsten Jöckel. Because of Wolfgang Jöckel's work as manager at one of the biggest manufacturers of shoe trees, the company can draw on more than thirty-five years of experience in this area. Besides the wholesale trade of furnishings, self-made shoehorns from plastics are the main product of the company. The shoehorns are available in many different shapes and in more than twenty colors. As a competent partner for specialized retail stores, Jöckel prints logos and advertising texts on shoehorns, shoe trees, and other articles according to the customer's wishes at the company's own print shop. Even laser engraving is possible.
www.schuhzubehoer.de

Ludwig Reiter

The shoe manufactory Ludwig Reiter was founded in 1885 by Ludwig Reiter as a shoemaker's shop. Today it is led in its fourth generation by the brothers Till, Uz, and Lukas Reiter as a family business with headquarters in Vienna. The staff of forty employees produces about 30,000 shoes per year by means of the "Goodyear process." In addition to the ready-made models, Ludwig Reiter also offers so-called private productions for which model, leather type, shoe lasts, and sole finish are determined by the customer. Other high-quality leather wares and accessories are also manufactured and various theater productions are equipped as well. After moving several times, in 2011 the headquarters—the whole shoe production as well as storage and administration—finally moved to the castle Süssenbrunn near Vienna, which had been bought and thoroughly renovated by Ludwig Reiter. A more stylish ambience for the manual production of traditional shoe and leather wares can hardly be imagined. Ludwig Reiter has sixteen of its own retail stores in Austria, Germany, and Switzerland, and two stores on franchise. For some time, high-quality shoe polish has also been distributed under the brand name Ludwig Reiter. www.ludwig-reiter.com

Keller Brushes

The Keller brush factory was founded in 1869 by Johann Baptist Keller and is now owned by the fifth generation of the family. At first the company specialized in woods for brushes; from the 1920s on, whole brushes were produced. Brushes for shoe care were integrated into the assortment at an early time, too. A special emphasis is put on high quality and long life. Products are made for everyday use and not for throwing away. Thus, a lifetime of thirty or even fifty years is not a rare thing. Raw materials are usually natural and environmentally friendly. The used wood is certified by the FSC (Forest Stewardship Council) and stems from ecologically sustainable cultivation. The product line is split into three groups: fine brushes, brushes for animal care, and household brushes, which include the brushes for shoe care. The vertical range of manufacture, after the delivery of material, adds up to 100%. This means, all steps of production are done locally on the site. Many brands have their brushes individually adapted and produced by the Keller brush factory.

www.keller-buersten.de

Kiwi

William Ramsay was born on July 6, 1868, in the Scottish city Glasgow. When he was ten years old, his family immigrated to Australia and settled in the vicinity of Melbourne. There his father established himself as a realtor. After finishing school, William joined in his father's company and later on, during a trip to New Zealand, came to know Annie Elizabeth Meek, whom he married in 1901. Then they moved to Carlton, a suburb of Melbourne. There he produced disinfectants and polishing agents together with his partner Hamilton McKellar. In 1904, Mr. and Mrs. Ramsay moved together with the entire factory to Elizabeth Street in Melbourne, where the production of a new shoe polish under the brand name Kiwi started in 1906. The name and the logo of the Kiwi bird was chosen to honor his wife's New Zealand origin.

At the beginning, William Ramsey rode in a horse coach from building to building and from village to village in order to sell his shoe polish. In a short time he could celebrate a big success in Australia. In 1912, after McKellar had left the company, Ramsay's father opened a subsidiary of the Kiwi Polish Company in London. A short time later, William Ramsey himself travelled to London to crank up sales in Europe. In 1914, he died of cancer. The First World War provided the company with its first big breakthrough. In 1917, the British army ordered 10,000 gross (1 gross = 12 dozen = 144) with a single purchase order, all in all 1,440,000 cans. By the end of the war, Kiwi was on the way to becoming a global brand. In 1924, Kiwi Polish was already sold in fifty countries, and during the Second World War the allied armies were quantity buyers. In 1967 Kiwi International was founded to consolidate the worldwide activities. In 1984,

Kiwi was bought up by the American major corporation Sara Lee, which in turn sold its entire line of shoe care products to the US-American company S.C. Johnson in April 2011. Today, Kiwi products are distributed in 200 countries and in Germany alone seven Kiwi articles are sold per second. With such a penetration of the market, it is no wonder that Kiwi is the global market leader. www.kiwicare.com

La Cordonnerie Anglaise

La Cordonnerie Anglaise [The English Shoemaker's Shop] is a French company located in Limoges, western France. Since 1895 shoe lasts and shoe trees have been made from wood, and for a couple of decades, also some from plastics. In the mid-1980s a line of shoe care products was started, which today is a complete assortment of care products and belongs to the best ones available. Besides hard wax pastes, emulsion creams, leather detergents, waterproofing, shoe care products for reptile leather, leather grease, and leather refresheners, there is especially one emulsion cream worth mentioning that is suited for cordovan. But the largest domain of *La Cordonnerie Anglaise* is the high-end range of shoe care items. Regardless of whether these are brushes, shoe care chests, or leather aprons, the most beautiful, most exclusive, and, of course, also most expensive tools usually stem from the "English Shoemaker's Shop."
www.lca-international.com

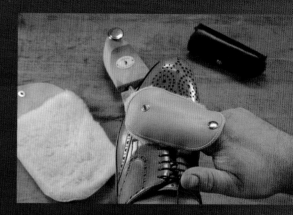

Polishing glove from lambs fleece.

An excellent assortment of brushes.

Various shoehorns for all occasions
are part of La Cordonnerie's
assortment.

Lederzentrum

The Lederzentrum [Leather Center] in Rosdorf near Göttingen, Germany, has existed since 1995. Back then, only two people were making leather repairs; now the company employs twenty-five people, has a sales volume of 3.6 million dollars [2.8 million euros], and sells its products globally. Thirty-five percent of the sales volume is earned with exports. The range consists of leather detergents, leather repair, and care products. These products are sold to the manufacturing industry (bags, cars, furniture, and clothing) as well as to museums, which also receive advice from experts of the Lederzentrum on how to maintain precious leather objects. Major customers, such as Bree, Volkswagen, Mercedes-Benz, and Bretz are supplied by Lederzentrum, as are, of course, thousands of private customers. With the exception of a saddler's and upholsterer's work, many kinds of repairs are done in-house—as long as the workshop isn't blocked by one of the many educational courses that take place each week. Here, the participants can learn about leather repair and the use of care products. Lederzentrum offers its own brands, *Colourlock* and *Leder Fein*, but also packages the brands of well-known manufacturers in the automotive industry and other industries. Under the name Elephant Leather Preserver, a type of leather grease is offered based on synthetic fats alone and is especially well-suited for the long-lasting preservation of furniture and car leather because it doesn't decompose. With respect to the ingredients,

the highest possible effectiveness in leather care is weighed against health considerations regarding the person using the product. This means, the product and the ingredients have to safely achieve the best-possible results for the leather. Spray cans and solvents are used only when they are absolutely necessary. High emphasis is put on best service quality and follow-up care.
www.lederzentrum.de

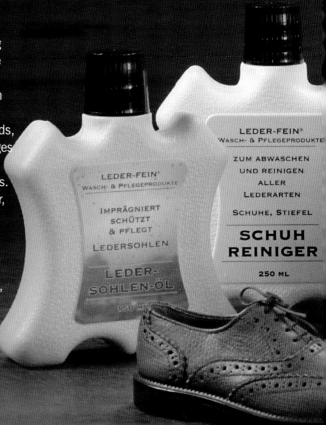

Colourlock has a perfect leather care program ranging from fat-dissolving agents to repair sets.

Lexol

The company Lexol initially came from New Jersey and was well-known for its good leather care product. In 1977, it was bought up by Summit Industries from Atlanta, Georgia, which still produces and distributes Lexol products. The original leather care product "Leather Conditioner," which is still produced today, was complemented in 1984 by a leather detergent and a leather care product for bright leathers called "Leather Dressing," which prevents a darkening of the leather. Since 2009, Lexol offers a 3-in-1 leather care product for occasional use, which at the same time cleans, cares, and protects the leather. It is especially suited for automobile leather. But, in general, all leather care products are appropriate for maintaining leather wares from smooth leather, including shoes, saddles, and automobile leather. They are delivered in various bottle sizes, in spray cans, and also as cloths. The latter are especially user-friendly during times on the road.

www.lexol.com

Lexol is best-suited for saddle care.

Pedag

Company founder Hartmut Schelchen started selling inlays, footbeds, and shoe care tools in 1955. Inside his garage, leather dye was filled from big barrels into small glass bottles for sale. From 1965 on, Hartmut Schelchen himself produced inlays in a former cow stable in Berlin-Charlottenburg because he was not pleased with the quality of the available wares, which were mainly imported. Distribution of the brand Eri followed in the 1970s. In 1975, HS Schuhbedarf changed its name to Pedag International, derived from the Latin name for feet, *"pedes."* Many years later he decided to gain a foothold in the area of shoe care, as well and to thus be able to offer a full assortment.

In 2003, the first shoe polish of "Pedag INTERNATIONAL" was launched in Germany and other countries. Today, the Schelchen GmbH Pedag INTERNATIONAL is a company located in the area of Berlin and employs more than 160 people. The company offers its products, including footbeds and soles, shoe care, shoe trees, shoelaces, and furnishings, worldwide. Within the large assortment of shoe care products, there is everything for the care of smooth and rough leather. With respect to the main ingredients, Pedag prefers natural ingredients, such as beeswax, lanolin, shea butter, and carnauba wax.
www.pedag.de

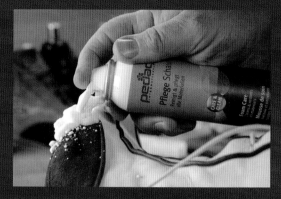

Pedag foam cleans and cares.

Poliboy Brandt & Walther

On January 1, 1930, Brandt & Walther GmbH was founded in Bremen, Germany, by Adolf Brandt and Otto Walther as a company for trading grain and imports. In 1935, a chemical department was incorporated and production of disinfectants and pest control agents started. In the following years, cleaning products and detergents were added, which were distributed under the name Polirol (derived from the expressions polish and oil). In 1951, the brand was renamed into Poliboy, because of the older rights of another brand. In 1952, the company moved to Lilienthal near Bremen, followed by the step-by-step extension of distribution all over Germany. The start of operation of their own R & D laboratory in 1967 marked the beginning of their own development of new products and the continuous refinement of already existing products. Today the company Poliboy Brandt & Walther GmbH, with its sixty-five employees, is still a family-led, middle-class firm. The assortment, which, by the way, is completely produced within Germany, includes—besides products for leather care—products for the care of furniture and floors, care products for silver, and several special cleansers. The brands distributed are Poliboy, Putzboy, and Schraders. In the area of furniture and silver care, Poliboy is the market leader in Germany and the products are distributed worldwide in thirteen countries.

The leather care products include an intensive care for leather, a leather cleanser, and moist cloths for the quick and simple care of leather. Besides the quality of the raw materials, such as beeswax, carnauba wax, and lanolin of mainly natural origin, Poliboy puts special emphasis on biodegradability of its end products and a large proportion of natural active substances, which also shows up in the new bio-product line. The company consciously refrains from using organic solvents and substances that are easily resorbed through the skin.
www.poliboy.de

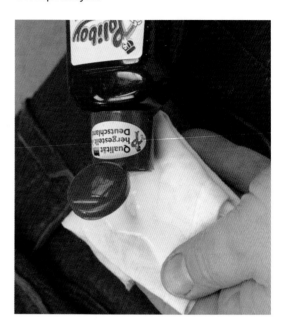

Poliboy care is also suited for handbags.

Royal Shoe Care

Royal Shoe Care was founded in 2006 by Kim Himer, Cologne. Royal Shoe Care offers shoe care boxes and chests for use at home, as well as a moveable shoe care cart and a shoe polish armchair for the commercial sector. All products belong to the high-end sector and are solely manufactured in Germany. The Royal Shoe Care Box is a small chest of solid construction with three pegged drawers, which incorporate a self-closing mechanism and in which the most important shoe care tools can be easily stowed. Because of the integrated handles, the box can be transported without problems.

The Royal Shoe Care Chest is a veritable piece of furniture that leaves nothing to be desired with respect to shoe care. In the upper area, under the drawer for dirt and debris, which can be opened sideways, there are a couple of small drawers for the care products

used for the most common leather types and dyes. In the center there are drawers for hard wax pastes and emulsion creams in all the color hues you can think of. And below that you'll find large trays for brushes, shoehorns, and replacement shoestrings. The work surface is covered with leather. Of course, all the drawers are tapped as well and supplied with a self-closing mechanism. For the box as well as the chest, exclusive woods are offered, such as Macassar ebony, Zebrano, walnut, walnut burl, rosewood, and bog oak. Other wood types can be specially ordered, if the customer wishes. Carry handles and other fittings are, as with the other shoe care furniture, either of stainless steel or brass.

The Royal Shoe Care Station is a roll cart designed especially for use in hotels with shoe care service. The work surface is at a comfortable height, made of glass, and can be cleaned easily after the work is done. In addition to the dirt drawer and the ten small drawers for stowing the shoe care products according to color, there are four lockable stock compartments in the area below. To make using the Royal Shoe Care Station easier, it is of lightweight, honeycomb construction and also has big rollers with ball bearings and locking brakes.

The Royal Shoe Care Chair was also developed for hotels, but also for shoeshine professionals who want to offer their customers an especially elegant and comfortable seat during shoe care. Besides various drawers for shoe care articles and two extendible trays, this "throne," which is furnished with burl wood and has a seat covered with leather, has two top-class features. In one armrest there is a cooler for champagne and in the other a humidor for cigars. Being cared for in this way, no customer

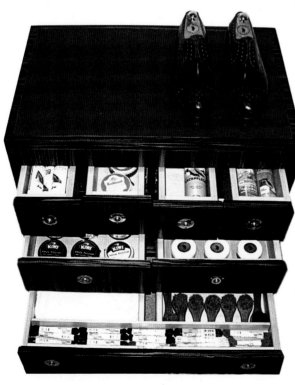

Royal Shoe Care Chair with a cigar humidor and cooled champagne.

will feel bored. But not just premium hotels that want to have a special eye-catcher in their lobbies, or especially ambitious shoeshine entrepreneurs, belong to this circle of customers. Some private individuals also indulge themselves with a Royal Shoe Care Chair. Besides this unusual shoe care furniture, Royal Shoe Care also offers a wide program of seminars for professionals and training with respect to shoe care. The seminars, which usually lasts from six to sixteen hours, are directed at shoe retail stores and hotel personnel in equal measure. www.royalshoecare.de

Lateral extension for placing care tools.

Saphir

At the beginning of the twentieth century, simple leather care and greasing agents under the name "Saphir" entered the market, especially in the military sector for items such as boots, belts, and tacks (saddles and harnesses). A high-quality care program was developed through intensive cooperation with the manufacturers of high-quality leather wares such as saddlers and makers of fine bags, later on with other shoemakers. At the world expo in Paris in 1925, Saphir won a gold medal for the exceptional quality of its products in the area of leather care. Until today, the original recipes have only been changed whenever legal requirements made this necessary. Today, Saphir is a brand of the company Avel in western France near Cognac. The company was founded in 1977 by Alexandre Moura and is headed by his son Marc since 2004. The products of Avel are exported to more than thirty countries. Avel produces shoe and leather care products for many well-known companies.

The products of the brand Saphir are divided into two lines. The standard series Saphir offers good care products for cleaning and maintaining leather wares and shoes.

The same goes for Saphir Medaille d'Or; it aims especially at the care for high-quality shoes. The items in this top product line are also partially suited for leather clothing, leather-bound books, and other leather wares. Only the best ingredients, such as carnauba wax, mink oil, and turpentine are used for Saphir Medaille d'Or. Saphir also offers an emulsion cream for cordovan, patent leather, and reptile leather, a universal leather-renovator, and a high-quality leather grease. In addition, there is a large assortment of shoe care accessories.
www.avel.com

Seeadler

Seeadler is specialized in premium shoe trees of the English style. The customers can choose their favorites from several ladies' and gentlemen's models either at the company's Internet shop or at upmarket specialized stores. With the exception of the lightweight plastic travel shoe trees, the materials used are the pleasant-smelling wood of the Canadian cedar, which is extremely resistant to fungi. This cedar is also used for building log cabins because it is said to endure for up to a thousand years. Also used is the unscented wood of the Asian guger tree. The shoe trees of the Victoria Edition, made from black tanned guger tree wood and having telescoping springs of a silvery color, plus appliqués, have an especially elegant appearance. Besides the materials, emphasis is put on the very detailed workmanship of the shoe trees and their functionality, which shows especially in the five-year guarantee—nowadays a real rarity. But not only product quality and choice—which, by the way, is quite straightforward because only fine shoe trees from solid wood are offered—provide for a steadily growing number of regular customers, but also a good cost-performance ratio.

www.seeadler.de

Seeadler travel shoe trees of plastics.

Swims

Swims is the brand of Norwegian designer John Ringdal. Besides loafers, jackets, and umbrellas, fashionable overshoes are the main product of Swims. As a Norwegian who grew up under unfavorable weather conditions and had inherited a pair of overshoes from his grandfather, John Ringdal was well-acquainted with using them and didn't want to give up the habit during a rainy stay in Paris. But he had to realize that their archaic appearance made him a target of jokes from his fellow students. In New York, which was pummeled by rain and snow and where he later lived for a while, the bad weather ruined several pairs of his high-quality shoes, which he couldn't do without in this fashion-conscious city. After searching for a suitable product to protect his shoes for several years, he decided to create modern overshoes himself. Today, Swims offers a multitude of different overshoes that

not only serve the classic taste, but also make allowance for fashion in color and finish. Women especially enjoy more than just the colors; the variety offered is extraordinary. For example, there are even overshoes for high heels. The exceptional product quality and the trendy realization provide the Swims overshoes with a unique feature that turn them into a product of choice for many women and men. www.swims-shop.de

Swizöl

The roots of Swizöl reach back to the 1930s when the Anwander family ran a drugstore in Zurich. In the drugstore, as well as the kitchen, Hans Anwander produced the first waxes and varnishes, initially for the maintenance of furniture. Since he couldn't find any product for the care of his automobile, he started to produce such care products himself.

Up to the present, all Swizöl care products are manufactured and packaged manually. Swissvax is the manufacturing company, which is headed by Claudius Anwander, grandchild of Hans Anwander, and co-owner Georg Weidmann. Swizöl nowadays offers a holistic product line for automobile and vintage car enthusiasts that leaves nothing to be desired, whether it is taking care of varnish, leather, or wheel rims. For each

case of cleaning or care, the appropriate means is available, produced from the best ingredients. Since Swizöl does everything to achieve the best-possible care result, it is no wonder that almost all manufacturers of luxury automobiles and many vintage car clubs swear by the products of Swissvax and it is known by insiders to be one of the best care lines worldwide. Of course, these products have their price, but they are worth it, according to the customers' opinions. Even individually produced wax for varnish care, uniquely produced for a special car of a certain color, can be made for the customer. With respect to leather care, the assortment is equally complete and outstanding, because Swissvax cooperates closely with the Lederzentrum in Germany.
www.swizol.de

Tapir

In 1983, Bodo Rengshausen-Fischbach founded the Tapir Wachswaren GmbH. As a student of ethnology, he was open to and interested in historical leather care and he chose the tapir as the company's symbol. The founder of the company restored old cars and realized that no care products existed for brittle and broken leather seats that met his expectations. During his research, he found an old recipe that he used as a basis for his first products. In the laundry room of his home, experiments were done on items with rare and exquisite waxes. As a result, the first care products were created. On the basis of these recipes, modern shoe and leather care products were developed. In the small manufactory at Dassel/Amelsen, Germany, between Göttingen and Hannover, high-quality, renewable, primary material such as natural waxes, oils, and solvents are used and the products carry a full declaration of all ingredients. During development, the company abstained from animal tests. The easy to use products are the result of extensive trials and their own best recipes. Petrochemical oils and waxes, aniline dyes, chemical solvents, and other raw material of petrochemical origin are not renewable and thus are not used. Today, besides the company owner, the two most important coworkers are also engaged in the business. Tapir offers products for the care of smooth leather, shoes for mountain-hiking, and coarse leather shoes, as well as leather oil and saddle soap.
www.tapir.de

Swing Time—Gallery for Art Déco Originals

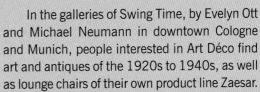

In the galleries of Swing Time, by Evelyn Ott and Michael Neumann in downtown Cologne and Munich, people interested in Art Déco find art and antiques of the 1920s to 1940s, as well as lounge chairs of their own product line Zaesar.

Everything started in 1988 with the trade and restoration of old, very high quality luggage from England. These restored and original pieces of baggage still comprise a core sector of the product panoply. Using their more than two decades of collected experience in the restoration of "vintage leather," work such as the refreshing of patina and the renewing of fittings is done very meticulously and in close cooperation with the customer. Suitcases and bags that have been restored this way—although they are ready for travel—are used by their current owners for decoration or stowing things at home instead.

For example, one bag might be used as an extravagant storing place for shoes and leather care products. Anyone interested in such original beauties of the finest quality will always find something at Swing Time.

www.swing-time.com

Tierowa

Tierowa has been a family-owned business for 100 years. Today, Ralf Mayer leads the fortunes of the company, together with his family. It all began around 1861 with his great-great-grandfather, who founded the firm. Ralf Mayer's great-grandfather, the master saddler Gastel, who owned a saddlery in Stuttgart, Germany, was already the supplier of the royal court of Baden-Württemberg in 1900. Around the same time, the firm changed more and more from traditional saddlery to sports saddlery. Grandfather Reinhold Mayer married Hedwig Gastel, the daughter of the master saddler, and in 1921, changed the sports saddlery of his father-in-law into a sports store that he named after the initials of his wife "Hedga." Since almost all sport equipment at that time, such as balls, skiing boots, or shoes for mountain-hiking, was made of leather, it didn't take long until "Tierowa intensive leather care" was developed as the first leather care product of the company and it is still available today. Generations of mountaineers swear by this excellent leather grease. You should know that after World War II, it wasn't unusual for people to tan leather at home. The need for leather care agents, as well as knowledge about them, was much greater than it is today. Since that time, connections with customers continue into the third generation. Grandfather Reinhold Mayer waits on the grandfathers of today's customers; and his son Heinz, father of the current company owner, brings in more customers.

As an educated agricultural engineer, Ralf Mayer has always been closely connected to nature and enthusiastic about soundly manufactured leather wares and articles of daily use. This enthusiasm is also the basis for Tierowa care products; the focus is on what is best for the leather. During the last twenty years, the assortment has continuously expanded to include leather cleaners, intensive waterproofing agents, and polish. Therefore, the business today is able to offer high-quality leather care products that have proven their worth for decades.

Tierowa was successfully used during expeditions in the Alps, the Himalayas and at the North Pole, in Alaska, and South America. The name Tierowa is derived from "Tierische Rohwaren" (animal raw materials), because to care for them is what the Tierowa products are made for.

Today, the company is located in Wiefelde, close to Oldenburg, in Lower Saxony, Germany.
www.tierowa.de

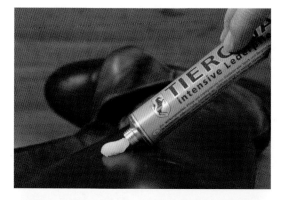

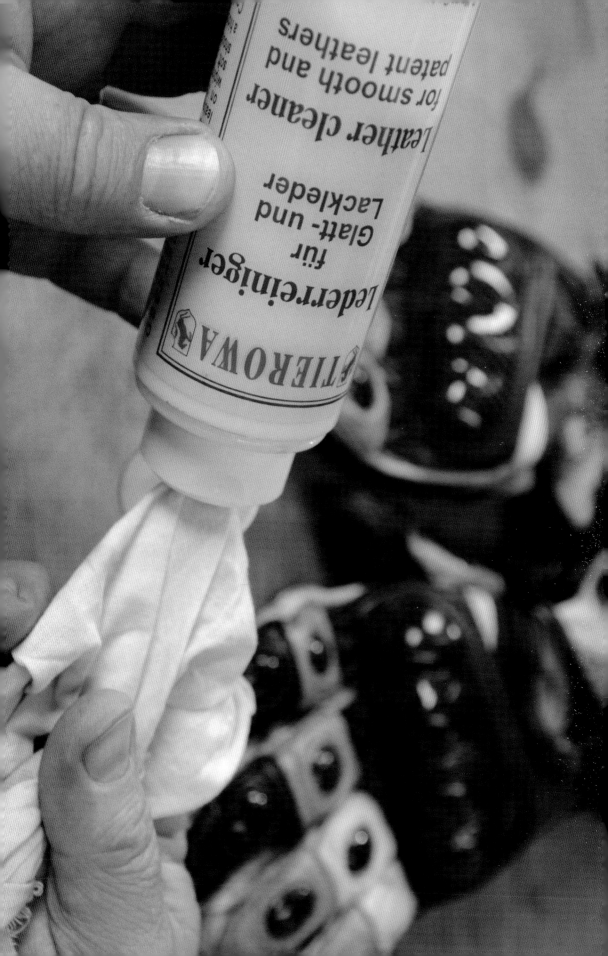

Tingley

The Tingley Rubber Corporation was founded in 1896 by Charles O. Tingley. He started by selling sealing plugs for bicycle tires. In proper style, he distributed them on his bicycle from his home in New Jersey to Buffalo, New York; Boston, Massachusetts; and Washington, D.C. In 1910 Charles Tingley welcomed William McCollum into the company as a business partner. The latter quickly started with an expansion of the products available and led the company with his commitment to quality and perceived product value. Together with his two sons, he thus laid the foundation for the company as it exists today. Meanwhile, Tingley designed the first rubber overshoe without lining and made it ready for the market by using the company's knowledge for processing rubber. This invention was the first step toward waterproof, protective footwear and clothing. Today, the family business is led by the fourth generation and offers several product lines of overshoes, rubber boots with and without steel toe caps, and rain gear for various industrial sectors, such as petrochemistry, the lumber industry, food industry, and office employees. Because of innovations and continuous improvements, Tingley's products still represent state-of-the-art technology.

www.tingleyrubber.com

Tonino

The company was founded by Antonio Visco in Cologne, Germany, in 1973 as a leather wares business with an emphasis on shoes. In 1996, the trained merchant Ciro Visco, son of the founder, took over the business. In 2005, he started selling shoe care products online, and since 2008 a line of leather and shoe care products exists under the brand name "Tonino." Special emphasis is put on natural ingredients. Thus, the company consciously abstains from the use of silicone and CFC.
www.Tonino1973.de

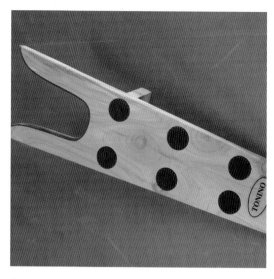

Bootjack of cedar wood by Tonino.

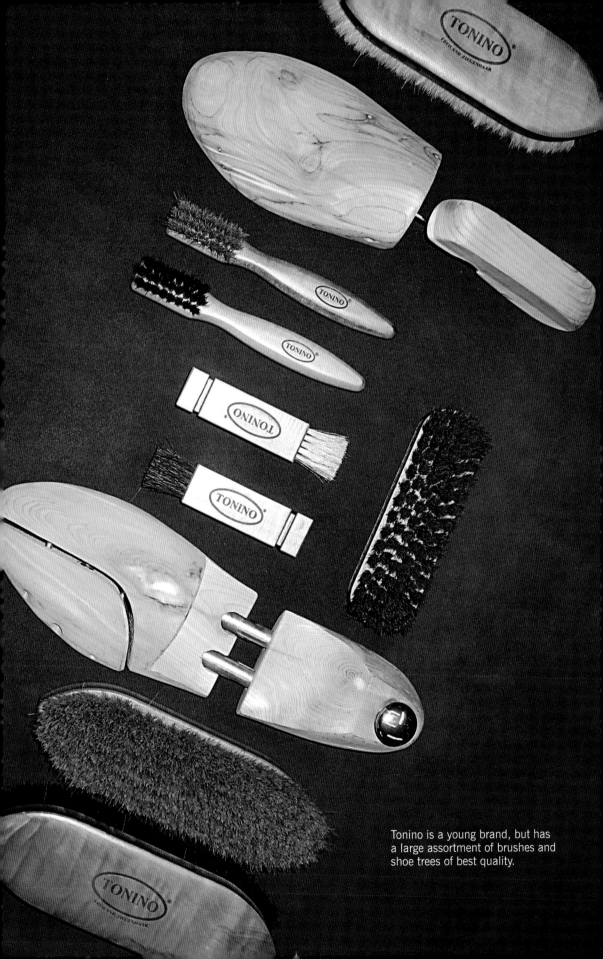

Tonino is a young brand, but has a large assortment of brushes and shoe trees of best quality.

Dr. Wack

Dr. Oskar Kurt Wack is a real pioneer and is known as the "Gyro Gearloose" of the care and detergent sector. In 1975, he became independent with detergents for AMC-pots (cooking pots made of stainless steel) after he had developed Mr. Clean at Procter & Gamble. An early milestone of the company was the development of the first detergent worldwide for tire rims of light metal. A car dealer who sold a used car to Dr. Wack wasn't able to perfectly clean the very dirty tire rims of that car. So Dr. Wack himself went to work and the result was the aforementioned detergent for tire rims. Via the care for cars and motorbikes, which at Wack has been one of the most important business branches from the very start, the way inevitably led to leather care about twenty-five years ago. The product "S100 *Lederpflege Glatt & Glanz*" [S100 Leather Care Smooth & Glossy] was especially developed for the care of heavily used motorcycle clothing and leather boots. At the end of the 1990s, A1 leather care for convertibles was added, initiated by the company's customer Porsche. This product, based on jojoba oil, has a natural sun protection factor of three to four and thus is especially suited for the protection of leather furnishings in convertibles against ultraviolet light. Over the course of time, the care program was enlarged with a waterproofing spray suited for leather as well as textiles; and the most recent product "S100 *Lederpflege Rau & Matt*" [S100 Leather Care Suede & Matte] has been on the market since 2011. It cares for and protects coarse leather and lusterless smooth leather, as well as leather-textile combinations. A washing agent for leather and textiles is also part of the assortment. To remove especially bad smells, such as that of moldiness, a special odor killer was developed that destroys the unpleasant odor molecules and does not just encase them. The product came into being because it was suggested by the reader of a motorcycle magazine. Bikers swear by products of Dr. Wack, and not only with respect to leather care.

www.wackchem.com

Bikers swear by the products of Dr. Wack.

Waldhausen

In 1836, Waldhausen GmbH & Co. KG was founded by Anton Waldhausen as a saddle shop in Cologne, Germany. By 1895, Waldhausen was regarded as the largest retailer of saddles and leather wares, and thus was promoted to become royal supplier for Emperor Wilhelm II. As early as 1911, saddles and other products were exported to other European countries. Despite the firm belief of Emperor Wilhelm II, who said "I believe in the horse. The automobile is nothing more than a passing phenomenon," from 1917 onwards the increased prevalence of automobiles and, starting in the 1920s, inflation both threatened the company's existence. In 1944, during the Second World War, the company was destroyed completely.

In 1945, Albrecht Assenmacher, Senior, started rebuilding the company. Harnesses, sample suitcases, and riding gear were included in the new products. In 1969, Waldhausen started production and distribution of saddles of the renowned Moll brand. In 1972, Waldhausen became official supplier of the German Olympic Committee for equestrian sport and it still holds this position today. Another expansion of the products is the brand ELT Paris, a leading brand of clothing for equestrian sport, which was purchased in 1989. In the year 2000, new headquarters in Cologne was begun, one of the most modern centers for the logistics of equestrian sport. Today, their assortment encompasses more than 12,000 items that are exported worldwide into sixty countries.

Waldhausen produced saddles for Jacqueline Kennedy and Luciano Pavarotti, too. For about thirty years, the company has offered leather care products for equestrian sport. Since 1979, Fafits is produced using an original recipe of Waldhausen—a paste for bootlegs made from natural materials that enhances adhesion of the boots to the saddle to provide better thigh stability and grip during show jumping. The entire Waldhausen care assortment includes leather cleaners, leather grease, leather oil, beeswax leather oil, and, of course, saddle soap, as well as boxes for care equipment and bags.
www.waldhausen.com

Woly by Melvo

Melvo produces and distributes shoe care agents and shoe furnishings for the brands Salamander, Woly, and Woly Sport. The company dates back to 1988 when Melvo Vertriebsgesellschaft mbH was created as a subsidiary of Salamander AG. In 1991, Melvo took over the Swiss brand Woly and continuously expanded over Europe and Asia. In 2002, the trading firm changed into a production company, because Salamander AG transferred the production of care products to Melvo. In 2004, the company was detached from the Salamander corporate group and since then has existed as an independent company. In 2009, a subsidiary was founded in Russia and a joint venture set up in India. Melvo took over the French LJW, with all its brands, in 2011.

The product lines of Salamander and Woly are a full assortment for all leather types and shoe care needs, including coarse and patent leather. Furnishings such as shoe trees, shoestrings, inlays, and shoehorns are also distributed under both brand names. Salamander offers some products for shoemakers, while Woly has an almost unlimited color variety of emulsion creams. Since even metallic color hues are available, these creams are especially liked by women. With Woly Natura, a shoe care product line is offered that is solely based on natural ingredients. Under the brand name Woly Sport, products for sports shoes are available, as well as waterproofing sprays and special washing agents for textiles.

The in-house laboratory is responsible for recipes and their improvement, thus providing a permanent quality assurance and product enhancement. The production takes place at the company's location in Ludwigsburg, Germany.
www.melvo.de

Woly offers various scents for shoe hygiene.

Care Products— Ingredients

The main ingredients of most of today's and yesteryear's shoe creams are waxes, which are responsible for the caring and conserving effects. Carnauba wax, montan wax (lignite wax), shellac wax, candelilla wax, and beeswax, among others, are used. To this add solvents, such as turpentine oil, which, depending on the amount, are responsible for the rather paste-like or ointment-like consistency. Natural solvents such as turpentine oil and limonene are increasingly used.

WAXES

Beeswax is a soft wax and, in shoe polish, is mainly used as a connective wax between the hard waxes used. Because of its low melting point of about 147 degrees Fahrenheit [64 degrees Celsius], it is flexible and assures that the applied care products don't get brittle. In addition, it has a waterproofing effect. Beeswax can be a yellow hue or a natural white, after it is cleaned of the dyeing pollen. Used in high dosage, it provides a pleasant smell to the caring agents, as long as it is not replaced by chemical substitutes.

Candelilla wax originates in Mexico and the southern part of the United States. It is secreted by the leaves of candelilla shrubs. It is hard, brittle, and of light-colored to yellowish hue. The melting range lies between 152–168 degrees Fahrenheit [67–76 degrees Celsius]. Candelilla wax in the shoe polish provides a high gloss.

Carnauba wax is the hardest natural wax and originates from the Brazilian carnauba palm. The very high melting range lies between 176–190 degrees Fahrenheit [80–88 degrees Celsius]. Of all waxes, carnauba wax provides the highest gloss and, because of its hardness, acts as a preserving agent. It is very expensive and much sought-after in the areas of leather and shoe care, as well as in the paintwork of cars.

Wax from oil palms is very cost-efficient. It absorbs scents very well and can hold them for a long time. Oil palm wax mainly originates from Indonesia and Malaysia. The problem with using this type of wax is its origin. In Southeast Asia vast parts of the rain forest are cut down in favor of oil palm plantations, which is the reason why some manufacturers abstain from using oil palm wax, despite its low price.

Montan wax is a mineral wax obtained from lignite. Ninety percent of the worldwide production stems from brown coal mining. Montan wax is very soft and is mainly used for reasonably priced care products.

Shellac wax is a very hard and gloss-providing wax from Southeast Asia and India.

Japan wax is the name for a mixture from various vegetable fats, such as the fat of the Japanese wax tree, and is not wax in the strict sense. The melting range lies between 125–129 degrees Fahrenheit [52–54 degrees Celsius].

SOLVENTS

Turpentine oil, also called **wood turpentine**, is produced by distilling the natural balm turpentine, which is mainly obtained from pines. It should not be mixed up with a cheap, artificial replacement for turpentine. The use of the expensive wood turpentine often marks the difference between a good and an excellent shoe polish. Wood turpentine can originate from a multitude of countries and is a natural solvent for waxes.

Limonene is produced from orange peel and is a natural solvent. It provides leather care agents with a pleasant smell of oranges and citrus fruits. It also has a strong cleaning effect. Limonene originates in the USA and South America.

White spirit, also called **mineral turpentine** or **turpentine substitute,** is a very reasonably priced petroleum ether, which is used as a replacement for high-quality turpentine oil.

Water is used as a replacement for solvents in emulsion creams, either in composite creams, which still contain solvents that are only partly replaced by water, or in water creams, which are completely free from solvents. Since, especially for pure wax creams, no high-quality hard waxes can be used anymore and the cleaning effects of the solvents are missing, these creams are always suboptimal with respect to their performance.

ADDITIVES

Stearin, as vegetable stearin, is obtained from palm oil and coconut fat, and, as animal stearin, is from animal fat. In contrast to paraffin wax, it is biodegradable, but also very expensive. It mainly originates in the area of Southeast Asia.

Paraffin wax is a by-product of crude oil extraction. Like stearin, it is added as a means to create the consistency of reasonably priced care products.

Lanolin or **wool wax** is obtained by washing sheep fleece and has a wax-like composition. Because of its ability to absorb water, it is used especially as an emulsifier in composite creams and water-based creams, but its qualities for care and waterproofing are also much appreciated characteristics.

Jojoba oil is not oil, but a type of wax. It is obtained from the fruits of the jojoba shrub, which has its home in the desert areas of Mexico and the southern United States. The wax protects leather from drying up, and thus keeps it soft and sleek. In addition, jojoba oil has good emulsifying qualities.

ENVIRONMENT AND HEALTH COMPATIBILITY OF CARE PRODUCTS

For allergy sufferers, we recommend a glance at the German magazine *Ökotest*, issue 11/2010. There, fifteen black, water-containing emulsion creams and four black, hard wax pastes were studied with respect to the environment and health compatibility of their ingredients. Unfortunately, the overall results are very bad. Seventeen creams contained carcinogenic polycyclic aromatic hydrocarbons, among them also naphthalene, which was detected in a very expensive hard wax paste. In many emulsions unhealthy preserving agents were found. With respect to the water-containing emulsions, the shoe cream Centralin was rated best; with respect to the hard wax pastes, Kiwi was best. Although this study surely offers good reference points for allergy sufferers, it has nevertheless to be taken into account that it is only a snapshot from the year 2010 and is only valid for the black shoe creams that were inspected. Other dyes may contain different chemicals and be of different composition. The study also tells you, on a secondary level only, about the useful qualities of shoe cream, such as gloss and care, since these were only weighted as thirty percent of the result. Also, the environmental burden of a single tank of gasoline in a small car is much higher than the lifelong use of hard wax pastes containing solvents such as white spirit.

With an average package content of about 1.7 oz. [50 grams] and a solvent proportion of about 65%, this results in 1.1 oz. [32.5 g] of solvents, with an amount of shoe cream sufficient for taking care of almost one hundred pairs of shoes. If compared to the tank size of a typical small car containing about 10 gallons [40 liters], then, roughly calculated, you end up with 1,230 cans of shoe polish of 1.7 oz. [50 g] each— an amount that would be sufficient for about 120,000 pairs of shoes. Have fun cleaning!

Types of Care Products

Shoe polish has the task of caring for leather, protecting it, and providing gloss to it. In general, two types are distinguished: the so-called hard wax pastes, which are made up of waxes, solvents, and dyeing substances, and emulsion creams for which water is used in addition.

Hard Wax Pastes

are always packaged in metal cans because they don't contain water, which could cause them to rust. In general, they are

suited for all shoes from smooth leather and provide protection and gloss. The portion of protecting and caring hard waxes is highest with them and because of their consistency they can be used very sparingly, which in turn compensates for the high price.

Emulsion Creams

are so-termed because they always contain water and thus make up an emulsion of fats and water. As a result, they have to be stored in non-rusting containers, such as glass pots and plastic tubes. Nowadays, some emulsion creams are also offered in plastic cans to evoke the appearance of hard wax pastes—which should not confuse you. Emulsion creams can also be used for smooth leather. Emulsion creams are divided into two types:

Mixed Emulsions

which contain water as well as solvents and

Water Emulsions

which only contain water and no solvents. Because of their—compared to canned creams—more fluid, ointment-like consistency, they penetrate deeper into the leather and thus are suited well for refreshing the color and penetrative care of the leather.

Although hard wax pastes are the first choice for high-quality shoes from smooth leather, about every fifth application a mixed emulsion cream should be used for penetrative care and refreshing the color.

Water, during production, is a cheap filling material and doesn't have any care or cleaning effects. But when using water, additional, actually superfluous chemicals, i.e. emulsifiers, have to be added. Accordingly you should abstain from the use of water emulsion creams.

Fluid Care Products

are usually colorless or milky and thus are suitable for leather clothing, leather accessories, leather shoes, and furniture leather. They consist of waxes, oils, and solvents.

Self-Shine Products

are based on silicone, or rather silicone oil. By coating with silicone, the leather loses its ability to breathe. Besides that, silicone has no effect on leather care and thus, especially for high-quality shoes, you should avoid using self-shine products. If used over a long period of time, they damage the shoe and shorten its lifetime.

Leather Oil

is a mixture of several oils to which some perfume and occasionally vinegar—because of its cleaning effect —is added. It is well suited for all types of leather ware, especially soft leather, and should always be used very sparingly.

Leather Sole Oil

is especially tuned for application to vegetable-tanned leather. Because of this, it should only be used on soles. Solvent-free leather sole oils can be used on the entire surface. If solvents are contained, the oil should not touch the seams of the sole, because these can be corroded and the bonding of the soles may become detached at the rim.

Care Products for Patent Leather

have a cleaning and shine-enhancing effect. They are available as fluids, foam, and sprays. They contain special softeners, which provide enduring elasticity to the leather.

Cleaning and Waterproofing Agents

Leather Soap and Saddle Soap

serve for cleaning all types of leather ware; it is also suited for furniture leather. But because of its strong re-greasing effect, it should not be used on coarse leather or horse leather (cordovan), since these leather types become greasy and lusterless, respectively.

Fluid Leather Cleaners

are available for smooth, coarse, and patent leather, and they are similar to leather washing agents and leather cleaning foam, simple in application and handling.

Waterproofing Aerosol Sprays

are usually based on fluorocarbon resins in connection with propellants such as butane or propane. The cheapest sprays are based on silicone, but are not very effective. Although the active substances are distributed finely and over a large area, half of it always misses the target. The penetration depth is also more shallow than that of a fluid waterproofing agent which is massaged into the leather by hand. If you bear in mind that about half of the content is made up of propellant and a spray can thus is only sufficient for a few applications, it is easy to understand that the effect of these sprays can be achieved by other care products in a better, more environment-friendly, and more cost-efficient way. At best, they can be used for quick renewal of waterproofing, but the price is correspondingly high. Whoever doesn't want to miss the fine spray effect can resort to environment-friendly vaporizers, which are usually smaller, but nevertheless last longer because of the missing propellants.

Fluid Waterproofing Products

are available in glass and plastic bottles with a sponge for application. They can be colorless or with a dyeing effect.

Leather Grease

should, because of its strong greasing qualities, only be used on rough-handled shoes, such as shoes for mountain hiking, work shoes, and hunting boots. It should always be used very sparingly and not too often because otherwise there is the danger of over-saturation with fats. Too much fat compromises the breathability and the leather can swell, which is especially unpleasant in extremely cold situations because the coat of fat can freeze on the shoes and thus sweat can't be transpired as water vapor.

Otherwise, leather grease may also be sparingly used on furniture, protective leather clothing, and car leather. And prior to using it next time, surplus fat should always be removed with a piece of cloth. Otherwise it can happen that the leather grease is transferred to the clothing.

Universal Care Products

consisting of a large proportion of wax and a small proportion of fat are often best-suited for maintaining rough-handled shoes because their small proportion of fat makes them easier for untrained persons to use.

Waterproofing spray for smooth and coarse leather.

Cleaning a classic Western saddle of a
museum done by Waldhausen in Cologne.

Shoe Polish Recipes for DIY

Creating your own shoe polish is interesting, instructional, and lots of fun. In addition, it is not very difficult in theory, but the devil is in the details. Specified amounts and temperatures have to be followed strictly. Thus it is recommended to purchase precise kitchen scales and a kitchen thermometer (best up to 302 degrees Fahrenheit [150 degrees Celsius]). Don't expect any miracles; even with very meticulous preparation, the result will not be as good as you are used to from commercially available shoe polish, especially not with the first try. After all, generations of chemists with a big budget and the possibilities of entire chemical facilities have worked on this before.

The basic process is composed of the following phases:

1. Melting the waxes
2. Dilution by means of solvents
3. Bottling/packaging
4. Post-treatment

The creams produced according to the following recipes can be packaged immediately after the dilution. Creams that have to be cooled separately prior to packaging are not taken into account here and also not the various methods of post-treatment. On a small scale, they are simply impractical.

Carnauba wax, white beeswax, and pigments.

Carnauba wax is poured into the warm oil.

The finished cream mixture is filled into a can.

Pigments are stirred inside the can.

The two following historic recipes originate with a chemist from the 1930s. The recipes weren't checked by the authors, especially not with respect to whether there are now dyes available that are easier to handle. If the temperatures are not kept exactly, the waxes may overheat or the wood turpentine evaporate and thus the relation of ingredients may not be correct anymore.

Historic Black Canned Cream

30 g carnauba wax
25 g raw montan wax
3 g soft ozokerite 136–40 degrees Fahrenheit [58–60 degrees Celsius]
66 g paraffin 118–122 degrees Fahrenheit [48–50 degrees Celsius]
12 g nigrosin oleate 1:2 (base)
360 g wood turpentine
pouring temperature 107–111 degrees Fahrenheit [42–44 degrees Celsius]

At first, the carnauba wax is melted in a water bath, because it needs a relatively high temperature for melting. Afterwards, reduce the heat slightly, add the raw montan wax, and melt it. Finally, melt the soft ozokerite at 136–140 degrees Fahrenheit [58–60 degrees] and the paraffin at 118–122 degrees Fahrenheit [48–50 degrees Celsius]. When all waxes are molten, stir them well and then mix in the nigrosin oleate (to achieve the color). In the end, add the wood turpentine in the center of the pot—don't pour it in at the rim, stir everything well, then fill it into cans.

Historic White Canned Cream

15 g paraffin, bleached
5 g carnauba wax, bleached
6 g montan wax
74 g wood turpentine

Again, first melt the carnauba wax in the water bath, then add the montan wax and melt it, after that add the paraffin, melt it, and stir everything well. Finally, mix in the wood turpentine and fill the mass into cans.

New recipe, tested by the authors and found to be good

5 g beeswax, bleached
5 g carnauba wax
5 ml ricinus oil
30 ml limonene
5 g pigment powder (for dyeing)
(e.g., earth-colors and theater-dyes, titanium oxide for "white")

First melt the carnauba wax in the water bath, then slowly reduce the heat, add the beeswax, and melt it. Stir well. Add the pigment powder and stir well again. Finally, mix in the limonene. Fill everything into a 50 g can and let it cool. Stir well every now and then until the mass has hardened to prevent the pigments from settling down at the bottom.

New recipe

2 g carnauba wax
5 g beeswax, yellow
3 g hard paraffin
0.5 g stearin
39.5 g wood turpentine

Melt the waxes in this order: carnauba wax, stearin, beeswax, then paraffin in the water bath, stir well, and let the mixture cool down a bit. Then mix in the wood turpentine. Fill the cream into a 50 g can and allow it to cool down.

The Historic Boot Polish of Lyon

Lyon's boot polish was well-liked in the nineteenth century because its gloss reputedly was not surpassed. In addition, it was very cheap and easy to produce. Of course, nowadays, even the cheapest shoe polish from the supermarket surpasses the shine and conditioning effects of this historic recipe by far. The original recipe reads as follows:

Parts	Ingredients
20	soap
10	oak apple
1000	water
60	potato syrup
10	starch flour
10	iron vitriol
30	bone charcoal (spodium)

Cook all ingredients, with the exception of potato syrup and bone charcoal, for an hour, then strain them through a piece of linen. Stir cautiously with potato syrup and bone charcoal—done.

ea cream

gs on our skin and not on leather. Nivea
n guarantees the creation of stains on
er.

ttermilk

e drunk and thus maybe cares for the gut
but surely not for the leather—at most it
ates mold inside leather.

nscreen

cts us from sunburns and belongs in every
aid kit, but not on car leather. Protection
nst UV radiation works differently for
er.

tter

gs on bread or in mashed potatoes; on
er it only creates rancid stains.

ve oil

y contains many unsaturated fats, is very
and healthy. But leather becomes overly
ated with fat by using edible oil.

nana peels

d be put whole into the bio trash can.
are not suitable as a replacement for
n; stains and mold on the leather threaten
sult.

• Urine for expanding leather

Generations of soldiers are said to have
practiced this, but simple warm water would
have been better. The uric acid just hardens
the leather. Special leather expanders are not
only better suited, but are more hygienic, too.

• Coal dust for blackening

makes a big mess, only dries out the leather
and scratches its surface.

• Car polish

is not suitable for patent leather. Although it
has a cleaning effect, it dries out the leather.

• White wine

To neutralize red wine stains by means of white
wine is simply nonsense! After the shock about
the red wine stains, you'd better drink the white
wine.

Leather needs competent and knowledgeable
care as well as nutrients, which are especially
matched to the tanning agents, oils, and
other chemical additives in the leather.

**For our readers, the aforementioned common
errors hopefully belong to the realm of bad
jokes from now on.**

Shoe Care

INTRODUCTION

Shoe care today can sometimes provide anti-stress therapy. Until the 1930s, well-heeled people's shoes were cared for by servants, however, today we are left to take up brush and cream, and not only in self-defense against mud and dust. The assortment of care products today is more extensive than ever before; yet the use of horsehair brushes and pastes for care has not been seen as compulsory work for a long time. For some career women and managers, grooming is more relaxing than relaxation exercises such as Tai Chi or Pilates. The action and reward is not only the relaxation of the nerves, but also a neat appearance.

Be cautious! Cheating doesn't help. Whoever wants to save themselves the effort and uses instant shoe gloss or similar products, which unfortunately are also part of the product assortment of renowned manufacturers, is in danger of virtually strangling their shoes. These instant shoe gloss products coat the surface in order to achieve a gloss effect. Unfortunately, this glossy surface is treacherous because it breaks during the rolling motion of the shoe and then reminds one of a broken sheet of glass rather than the surface of a well-cared-for shoe. People caring for their shoes can be divided into three types:

1. THE IGNORAMUSES

Lack of knowledge and laziness are probably the reasons why shoe care is not of interest to them. They often prefer cheap footwear and as means for care at most some instant shoe polish à la Glitzi is considered.

2. THE PRAGMATISTS

Pure economy urges them toward care, because they know that cleaning shoes serves the longevity of the footwear. Without an emotional stake, they go for brand names and complete the maintenance program with the precision of a Swiss watch.

3. THE AESTHETES

Probably the smallest group, but also the most inquisitive and meticulous one, is always on the search for the best care products and tools. Perfectly equipped, these people start the work and not only invest money, but also time in the best care for their leather treasures. As a reward for the invested time, money, and sweat, they have a longer service life and guarantee a stylish and neat appearance. Shoes for them have an iconic status, and care is virtually declared to be a science. Thus it can happen that an aesthete, as a real care specialist, has more knowledge and proficiency than some of the shoemakers.

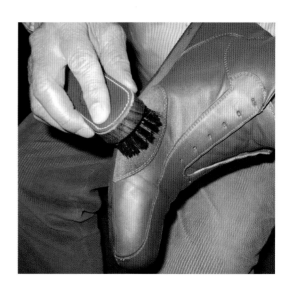

Race driver legend Jochen Mass caring for his calf leather race driving shoes. He belongs to the group of pragmatists. The shoes are cleaned and cared for, but without making a science out of it.

In the hope to convert some of the ignorant, to give additional tips to the pragmatists, and to confirm the aesthetes, we now show in great detail how to optimize care step-by-step in order to reach the Shoe Care Olympus of respectable shine.

First of all, you should only buy good footwear, because all the scrubbing and polishing doesn't help if the quality of the leather isn't up to it. But only with the right care products will you achieve the elegant shine that signals your counterpart that he/she is facing a neat or even noble person. Cleaning shoes also makes sense ecologically. It not only enhances the attractiveness of the footwear, but also creates a close relationship with the shoe and thus causes the person wearing and caring for the shoes to give them a closer look. This close look teaches us to recognize the need for shoe repairs early enough, which also helps to oppose the trend toward quick disposal of shoes. Several hundred million shoes end up in the trash can each year because our throwaway society quite often doesn't have an eye for care and repair possibilities of shoes. A longer shoe life in the long run helps in combating the trash-mountains of our affluent society. Thus, cleaning shoes is ecologically innocuous; however, you should take a look at the ingredients of the care products—although bio-products don't always have to be first choice.

If you want to achieve a good result with shoe care, you need some time. For lazy people it is helpful to introduce a few rituals and to keep in mind some things.

Here are a few tips

1. THE PLACE FOR MAINTENANCE SHOULD BE WELL LIT.

2. CLOTHING SHOULD BE PROTECTED BY AN APRON; HANDS WITH DISPOSABLE GLOVES.

3. ALLOW FOR SUFFICIENT TIME.

4. HAVE ALL NEEDED TOOLS AT HAND.

5. USE OLD NEWSPAPERS AS A WORK SURFACE.

6. PUT THE SHOES TO CLEAN NEXT TO EACH OTHER.

7. DETERMINE A SPECIAL DAY FOR MAINTENANCE; e.g., SATURDAY OR SUNDAY.

8. PLAY YOUR FAVORITE CD; IT'S MORE FUN WITH MUSIC.

9. INVITE FRIENDS AND CARE FOR SHOES TOGETHER.

These are only a few possibilities of many. In the end, everybody decides according to his/her own taste. In the long run, as with sports, the best results come from motivation. Regardless of whether you are an aesthete or a pragmatist, are crazy about beautiful patina or simply want the shoes to live longer: with the right know-how the footwear will be protected against quick aging even with the most sparing care effort

symbol
upper material

symbol
tread sole

symbol
lining and insole

symbol
leather

symbol
coated leather

symbol
other materials

The European Guideline for Shoe Designation

This guideline has been valid in Germany since 1997. It divides shoe parts into four material groups for the upper material, tread sole, lining, and insole, which are all represented by their own symbols:

UPPER MATERIAL
TREAD SOLE
LINING AND INSOLE

LEATHER
Tanned skins and furs whose fiber structure has not been changed are called leather. Finely milled leather strips mixed with glue are not classified as leather.

COATED LEATHER
Coated leather has to have a layer of dye or foil that is at least 0.15 mm thick and is not allowed to be more than a third of the overall thickness. Otherwise it is called uncoated (if the layer is thinner) or is counted to the artificial leathers (if the layer is too thick).

OTHER MATERIALS
All materials that don't belong to any of the other groups.
It is not required to mention which materials are used. There are also no statements about which chemicals were used during production or are still contained in the product.

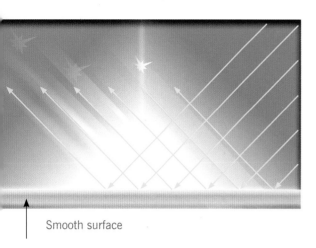

Smooth surface

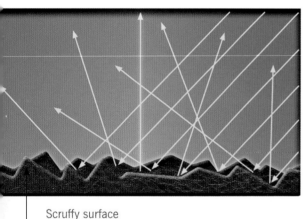

Scruffy surface

Leather
Polished shoe cream surface

Why Leather Shines

When light meets a smooth surface, shine is created by its reflection. All light rays are reflected in accordance with the physical law that the angle of incidence is equal to the emergent angle and thus the rays are reflected at the same angle but in the opposite direction. This reflection of the light rays is perceived by our eyes as shine. The smoother the surface, the more intense is the gloss effect. A rough surface, as with that of scruffy leather, looks like a mountainous landscape under the microscope. If it is met by light, the light is reflected by the many "mountains" and "valleys" into many different directions and thus the surface is seen by the eye as being dull. If the "valleys" are filled with a caring agents, a relatively smooth surface is created, though not a really smooth one. Thus a surface with a faint luster is created. If the surface is then polished, it is ground flat by this process and the desired high gloss effect is created. Waxes that may be contained in the care product are melted by the frictional heat and form a surface as smooth as glass, which enhances the effect even more.

Here you can easily see the difference between a scruffy cordovan shoe and a polished one and that it is reasonable to keep shoes in shape by means of a shoe tree.

Brushes and Tools

All brushes and tools should always be of good quality. These things have to be functional and have a long service life. When properly used, high-quality brushes can work for more than fifty years without problems and shoehorns almost indefinitely. In general, convenient handiness and, especially with brushes, the materials and workmanship are decisive. It is thus recommended to not save money during the purchase. New brushes lose hair during the first few times you use them; this is normal and no sign of bad quality.

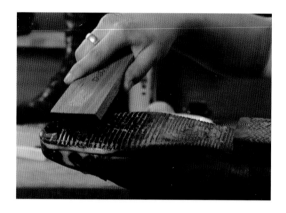

Shoe Cleaning Brushes

A shoe cleaning brush is especially indispensable for rough-handled shoes. Usually the bristles are not as close together as with other brushes. Bristles of strong, robust natural fibers, such as Tampico Fiber—also called Mexico fiber—which is made from the leaf fibers of agaves or pig bristles, are optimal. Artificial fibers have sharper edges and therefore are less suited for especially fine and soft upper leather.

Application Brushes

The simplest and best method to apply shoe polish is by means of shoe brushes. Each color should have its own brush. For leather types with a relief-like surface, such as Scotch grain, but also for the area of the seam between bootleg and sole they are suited best. There are two types of shoe brushes, ordinary brushes with the handle perpendicular to the bristles, and brushes with the handle attached in line with the bristles. The latter enables the user to reach the bottom of a pot without problems. This means that with the usual shoe brushes, emulsion creams can't be used up completely. High-quality shoe brushes are equipped with horse hair. Special narrow shoe brushes are superfluous because the usual shoe brushes are already small enough to get into all the hard to reach areas. If the brushes are clotted with old shoe polish, they can easily be cleaned with warm soap suds or some dishwashing detergent.

Shoe Polishing Brushes

Polishing brushes are available in many sizes and shapes; here the preference of the user is decisive. But it is important that the size of the polishing brush is not too small in order to enable long, uniform movements. With these the results are best because the longer contact between the leather and the brush raises the frictional heat, which in turn melts the waxes of the shoe polish and creates the luster. The best polishing brushes are made with horsehair from the tail.

The soft-as-silk, highly dense brushes from yak or goat hair are especially well-suited for fine polish. There should be a separate brush at hand for light and dark colors.

Brushes for Coarse Leather

Coarse leather brushes are divided into brass brushes for velour leather and brushes from caoutchouc or rubber for nubuck. Brass

brushes are too aggressive for nubuck leather because nubuck is not ground as much as velour. Brass brushes are either available as brushes with brass bristles only for napping, or in combination with a rim of other bristles, which provides a cleaning "sweep effect." The brass bristles are made of corrugated brass wire; they provide the best elasticity as well as adhesion. High-quality brass brushes have rounded wire ends, which don't damage the leather with cuts, as can happen with brushes of inferior quality.

Brushes for nubuck are supplied with caoutchouc, rubber, or pig bristles. These materials are absolutely sufficient for roughening and cleaning nubuck. But brushes with caoutchouc bristles wear out quicker. As an alternative solution you can consider small brushes with rubber knobs on one side and brass wire on the other. But, although they are suited equally well for velour and nubuck, their application is, because of their small size, not satisfying.

Leather Erasers

Leather erasers are available as pure coarse leather erasers or as universal erasers for smooth and coarse leather. The application is similar to that of an ordinary eraser. The effect is usually very good and immediately visible, but the treated area has to be cared for or waterproofed again.

Cleaning Shoe Brushes

Many people probably throw encrusted shoe brushes into the trash can. But this doesn't have to happen because they can be easily cleaned. **Caution:** don't leave these brushes in the water for too long because then the wood starts to warp and the bristles fall out.

Pour very hot water with dishwashing detergent into a receptacle.

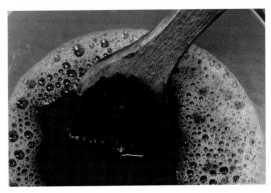

... then clean the dark brushes.

First clean the light-colored brushes...

Dry the brushes with a kitchen cloth.

Now the brushes are ready for the next use.

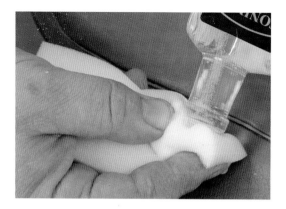

results can compete with the gloss created by a polishing tool prepared like this. By means of the nylon, the highest-possible frictional heat is created, the waxes melt, bond together, and result in a mirror finish, which almost reaches that of patent leather, especially if the shoes are made of cordovan.

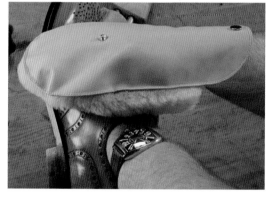

Rags, Cloths, Sponges

Instead of using shoe brushes, as alternative means for applying shoe polish leather rags, textile cloths, or application sponges work well. Which of these is used depends on your own preference. Textile cloths should be washed prior to first use in order to avoid unnecessary lint. Best suited for such use are cloths from microfiber or cotton. Sponges are especially well suited for shoes made from braided leather or when using saddle soap. The leather rags are made of chamois-tanned shammy and can be used for cleaning windows as well.

Nylon Stockings

Anyone who wants to achieve the ultimate polishing gloss wraps the polishing brush in a piece of cloth, covers it with a nylon stocking, and fastens it well with a knot. There is no brush, regardless of the type of bristles, whose

Polishing Gloves

Polishing gloves are an alternative to the polishing brush. Besides personal preferences, they make sense especially for braided shoes or bicolored Spectator models, but also for shoes made of a leather-textile material mix. By the almost direct contact of the fingers with the shoes, polishing can be done more exactly than is the case with a polishing brush. The second advantage is the smaller force necessary, which becomes noticeable especially in case several pairs of shoes have to be polished consecutively. The gloss effect is somewhat less, especially when compared to a brush with nylon stocking, because the polishing glove doesn't create as much frictional heat.

Whether the glove is made from textile, microfiber, or an especially classy leather with a lining of lambs fleece is a matter of taste. Because of its dense pelt structure, the latter is especially well suited for fine polish, refreshing polish, and for very sensitive upper leathers as well as shoes from patent leather. A separate glove is needed for light, medium, and dark colors.

Shoehorns

Shoehorns are probably "the" shoe care utensil that most people visually response to. Correctly considered, shoehorns are shoe care products because if they are never used, sooner or later an "accordion heel" will be the result. If this has happened already, the shoe is a total loss; it is irreparably damaged.

Virtually all shoehorns are functional, regardless of material or shape; even a tablespoon would be suitable. Anyone who cannot bend down easily may use a very long one, which is used to put shoes on while standing. And anyone traveling can take a small, lightweight travel shoehorn with them.

But, since shoehorns usually are kept at the coat rack, visible to all, and are also offered to guests, their appearance is very important. Probably the most beautiful ones are made of zebu horns and are produced in Great Britain with intricate hand work.

Shoe Trees

Shoe trees can basically be divided into two categories. On the one hand, there are the custom-made shoe trees that match the feet of the person wearing custom-made shoes and thus fit best into these shoes; on the other hand, there are the serial shoe trees, which are offered in various average sizes, the so-called ready-made sizes.

In both cases, their function is to simulate the foot and to thus keep the shoe in shape, reduce wrinkles caused by walking, and to take pressure from the bottom construction. They have to be put into the still warm shoes immediately after taking them off. Because of body heat and sweat, the leather expands during wearing. During drying and cooling, it shrinks again and adapts to the shoe tree. To let this process work best, the shoes should stay at least twenty-four hours, better forty-eight hours, on the shoe tree.

High-quality shoe trees are made from wood and, if they are not varnished, take in sweat or moisture from the leather, supporting drying. For better air circulation, the front part of the shoe tree often has holes or slits. Varnished shoe trees may sometimes look prettier than the ones without finish, but these can't take in any moisture. The shoes dry more slowly and with very wet shoes a film of water may be created between the leather and the shoe tree. This is not only unhygienic, but also doesn't do well for the leather. The wood used on unpainted shoe trees either stems from beech trees or western red cedar, both of which give off an especially aromatic scent because of their essential oils. This scent evaporates after a while, but the anti-bacterial effect nevertheless stays.

Foam shoe trees for pumps by Nico.

Bootleg stretchers prevent accordion wrinkles.

Seeadler plastics and varnished, light wooden shoe trees.

Production of shoe trees at La Cordonnerie Anglaise [The English Shoe] in Limoges.

For keeping shoes in shape, shoe trees from solid wood that not only fill the front part of the shoe but also the heel are best suited. In general, they are connected by two telescope springs and quite often the front part is divided in two by telescope springs and thus the front part of the shoe is completely filled. The springs must always have the correct size, because otherwise the shoe may be either stretched too much or not filled completely. For shoes that are put onto shoe trees whose front part is not divided, the fit of the shoe tree has to be corrected by hitting it sideways and not too hard against the side of the big toe in order to make it fit tightly against the leather.

Screwed shoe trees can be brought to exactly the right length and tension by means of a metal thread. Unfortunately, they don't fill the heel completely. Hinged or foldable shoe trees are made from solid wood and have a hinge in the center, by which the heel part is folded into the shoe after putting the front part in first. This type of shoe tree is especially well suited for custom-made shoes, if they were made in the shape of the shoe last.

With wooden shoe trees consisting of three parts, the front part is put into the shoe first, then the heel and finally the central, wedge-shaped part is put in between. The deeper you press it between the other two parts, the higher the tension and the shoe is held perfectly in shape over its entire length.

You had best abstain from using shoe trees with coil springs because the heel isn't filled completely and the tension, depending on the shoe, is either too high or too low.

In general, the tension should be such that the shoe tree has a tight fit without the shoe is being overstretched. If the sole takes on a concave shape—which happens if the shoe tip faces downward, the tension is too high.

Plastic-velour shoe trees may be found, especially for ladies' shoes. For pumps these act as pure stretchers for the front part only. Since patent leather is often used for ladies' pumps and the shoe leather is thus not breathable, plastic shoe trees don't have a disadvantage here. In addition, they are much lighter than wooden shoe trees, which is especially pleasant during times of travel.

Bootleg stretchers in use.

Caution: shoe trees with springs can overstretch shoes.

Shoe trees of solid wood are available from beech wood, cedar wood, or poplar, lacquered as well as in countless variants without varnish.

Shoe Hygiene System and Dryer by Therm-ic

Moist shoes are not loved by anyone. Shoes should not only be dry, but also hygienically clean with a pleasant smell. This is the ideal field of application for the shoe hygiene system of the company Therm-ic. This innovative product dries rapidly and quietly, provides a clean inner environment for shoes and gloves by means of UV-light and shoos away unpleasant smells with special, scented leaves.

The speed of the drying process can be set as well as the temperature. Another selling point: the timer—this way it is easy to program when the device should end its work. www.thermic.com

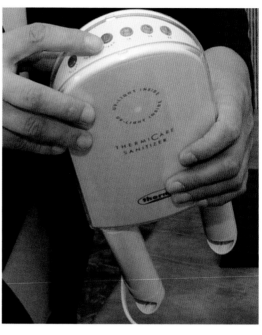

The dryer is very easy to use.

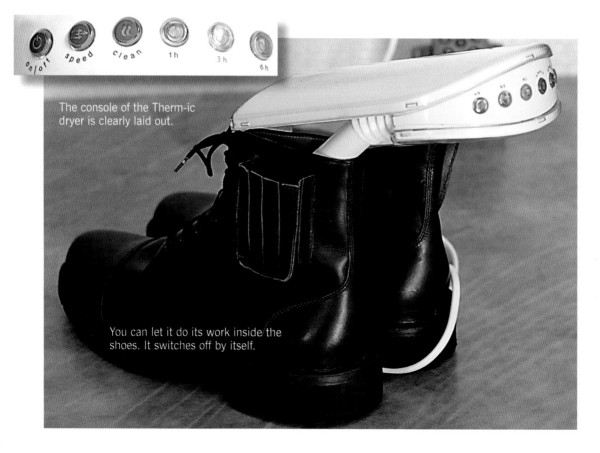

The console of the Therm-ic dryer is clearly laid out.

You can let it do its work inside the shoes. It switches off by itself.

Galoshes—Overshoes

The expression "galoshes" stems from the Latin *"solea gallica"* which means "Gallic sandals." Today, galoshes is the term for a pair of overshoes made of rubber. They are especially widespread in North America and their function is to protect the actual footwear from moisture, snow, and dirt. People who wear high-quality leather shoes in everyday life and necessarily have to expose them to dust and dirt quite often especially appreciate the value of galoshes. Thus, they are well-liked by architects and veterinarians who have to work on construction sites and stables, respectively, on a regular basis. Overshoes are light, foldable, easy to handle, reasonably priced, and provide good grip on almost any substrate by means of their profile-like soles. Whoever had a pair in the car, at work, or at home at any time, surely does not want to do without their use and their shoes won't be harmed by any kind of weather anymore. In addition, the airtight rubber galoshes have a warming effect, which is especially valued by their owners during cold weather. Galoshes are available for all kinds of shoes and boots, even for ladies' pumps. They are a real means of shoe care.

Swims also delivers a cleaning pad.

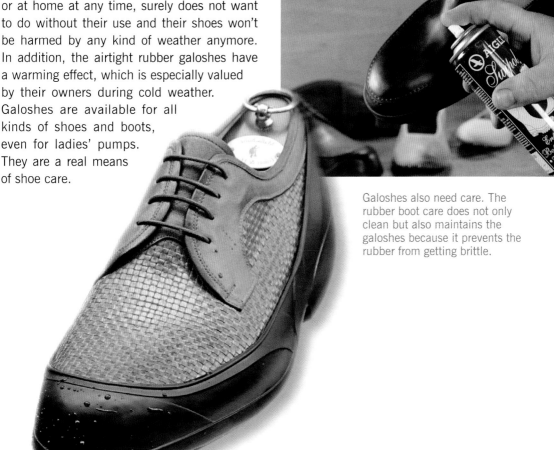

Galoshes also need care. The rubber boot care does not only clean but also maintains the galoshes because it prevents the rubber from getting brittle.

Shoebone / St. Hugh's Bone

A shoebone is a bone from the front leg of a deer; in the English language it is often referred to as "St. Hugh's bone" or simply "deer bone." It is used for removing scratches from leathers processed on the flesh side, such as cordovan (see page 140, care of cordovan shoes). This bone is said to contain enough bone oil itself to prevent too high a friction and thereby further damaging of the leather. Whether this really has to be a bone and whether or not another rounded, smooth item could be used remains to be seen.

The legend describes the origin of bones as a shoemaker's tool as follows:

Hugh, son of Aviragus, king of present-day Wales, was born in the third century A.D. He married the Christian princess Winifred of Flintshire and soon converted to Christianity.

As a result, he was repudiated by his father and from then on lived in poverty. During the daytime he preached the Christian faith and in the evenings, during his spare time, he worked as a shoemaker. Both were sentenced to death for demagogery around 300 A.D. Before he was hanged, his friends stood guard in front of the prison and consoled him. Because he didn't have any money he could leave to them, he is said to have willed them his bones in order to make tools for shoemaking from them. According to legend, this indeed happened, which is the reason why the expression "St. Hugh's bones" for all kinds of shoemaker's tools was very common for a long time in Great Britain. The legend of St. Hugh was incorporated by the British novelist Thomas Deloney in the drama *The Gentle Craft* in 1597.

The shoebone is used for repairing scratches on smooth leather.

Hand-held Shoe Polishing Machines

Nothing is more superfluous than a hand-held shoe polishing machine, regardless of whether it is powered by batteries or an electric cord. In times of energy shortages, it is clear that these are morbid outgrowths of our dependence on technology. We tried our luck nevertheless, with the result that the antique Peugeot device from the 1960s now functions better than the modern machines.

It is delivered with creams that reeks so much of gasoline that the best leather probably surrenders faster than you think.

Qixer Shine delivers the cream within the pad, if you are lucky. Three out of four pads were delivered already desiccated.

Polishing works, thanks to a strong motor, but is nevertheless not as good as a manual polish.

Even with light pressure, the Qixer Shine stops. You can polish manually just as well from the start.

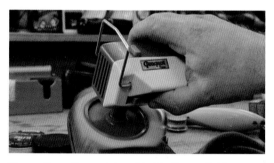

The antique Peugeot hand-held shoe polishing machine from 1960 has enough power for creaming.

Stand-alone Shoeshine Machines

They often stand in hotels, likely in the restroom area. Have you ever thought about what the person before you rubbed into the brush (street dirt, dog droppings, or even urine)? Who wants to have this on his/her upper leather, not to speak of the care that doesn't take place anyway! We don't want to write more about this topic.

Peugeot original instruction manual of 1960.

Practical Application

"Old friendships and good shoes need the most care," a proverb says. Having said this, we now start to work.

Shoes from Patent Leather

For thorough care, the shoelaces should always be removed first. Whether or not you leave the shoe tree in the shoe during care is a matter of personal taste.

First, the shoes are cleaned with a shoe cleaning brush or a moist cloth.

Only with very dirty shoes do you take up some leather soap or saddle soap with the moist cleaning brush and brush the entire shoe, including the soles with the wet soap suds. It is important that the entire shoe comes in contact with the water because otherwise water stains are created during drying. Caution is needed for very fine upper leathers; here you ought to use a sponge. Afterwards, the shoe is rinsed under running water. The shoe care aesthetes apply a mixed emulsion cream to the moist upper leather that permeates into the leather during the drying process and thus provides penetrating care and refreshes the colors. Here, too, it is important that the entire shoe is treated with emulsion cream. But this whole procedure is only necessary for extremely dirty shoes or the most demanding standards. After this cleaning process, the shoe is stuffed with newsprint and dried overnight at room temperature. The newsprint can be exchanged several times as soon as it has become moist; this will quicken the drying process. Shoes with leather soles are always put on their side in order to allow the sole to air-dry.

In case a dry cleaning was sufficient, you can continue immediately. Now hard wax paste or emulsion cream is applied thinly with a shoe brush. Apply the shoe cream lightly several times and polish, rather than applying it thickly once—the result speaks for itself. With the shoe brush, the shoe polish can be massaged into the leather well and you can also reach areas that are not easy to access, such as the holes of brogue shoes and the edge between the bootleg and the welt.

For the shine, a canned cream is preferable; it doesn't contain water and has a higher content of protecting waxes. But if you wish to refresh colors while providing penetrating care, your choice should be a high-quality mixed emulsion cream that also contains solvents. Because of its more fluid consistency, it penetrates deeper into the leather. But the penetration depth is also dependent on the duration. Thus, you should wait at least fifteen minutes with an emulsion cream and about an hour when using a hard wax paste before you start polishing. This waiting period is important to allow the oils to be absorbed, the solvents to evaporate, and the waxes to harden. Prior to polishing, the residual shoe cream is massaged into the leather once more and then the excess cream is picked up with a cloth. Now you polish, either with a microfiber polishing cloth, a polishing brush with horse hair bristles, or, best, with a polishing brush covered by a nylon stocking. If you moisten the brush with a bit of saliva, you'll achieve a more intensive gloss, virtually a "water gloss polish" done at high speed. By means of the enzymes contained in the saliva, the shine is even better than that achieved by using water. Thus, the highest gloss is achieved and, at the same time, the best protection, too. The fanatics among the shoe care aesthetes clean the shoes several times in a row to achieve the highest mirror gloss, or they first apply an emulsion cream and then the hard wax paste once more. After the polish, you can polish again with a fine polishing brush of horse hair, goat hair, or yak hair in order to achieve the ultimate gloss.

Cordovan Shoes

Because leather processed from its flesh side doesn't have a smooth surface, this has to be achieved artificially (with cream wax). Thus, it is also possible to recreate it after damage. An emulsion cream suitable for cordovan is applied on top of the scratches and is then rubbed into the leather with high pressure by means of a shoebone. Afterwards, the area is smoothed with emulsion cream using slight pressure and circular movements. This way the uniform surface is restored. Then, hard wax paste is applied and the surface is polished. Whoever really wants to distinguish themselves when polishing their cordovan shoes takes the time-intensive effort to treat the entire shoe with the bone or uses "water gloss polish."

Caution: Don't use saddle soap. Because of its re-greasing effect, it is not suitable for cordovan.

The best horse leather originates from Horween in Chicago, Illinois. Nobody achieves such a glossy depth as these Americans who have been producing cordovan leather since 1905. Horween was founded by the Ukrainian immigrant Isadore Horween.

Water Gloss Polish

As an alternative to the classic high-gloss polish, for shoe care aesthetes the water gloss polish is suitable. For this, first hard wax paste is applied, which you allow to absorb for about an hour. Afterwards, excessive paste is removed with a cloth and then a polishing cloth is wrapped around two fingers. It is important that the surface at the finger tips, with which the polishing is done, be as smooth as possible. Only this way is the needed water film between cloth and shoe created. Now you take up a bit of hard wax paste and moisten the shoe with a few drops of water—best by means of a cloth. And then you polish with slight pressure. When the water is polished away, you again take up a bit of hard wax paste and moisten the shoe with a few drops of water.

By means of the water film and frictional heat, the shoe cream is distributed in an optimal way and smoothed. The already cared for surface is not attacked by the water film, and each ever-so-small groove and wrinkle is provided with shoe cream. As a result, a surface smooth as glass is created. The whole procedure takes about ten minutes per shoe. Afterwards the shoe is left to harden for a few hours and then receives its final polish, best with the nylon-covered polishing brush again. The water gloss polish provides the highest shine and is very durable. It can be refreshed quickly by some polishing with the fine polishing brush and some saliva.

Caution: The water gloss polish only works with hard wax polish from a can, only this provides the necessary watertight surface!

All waxes are removed by cleaning.

Sometimes tanning fat emerges on the surface. This is no blemish and you can simply wipe it off.

After cleaning, apply cordovan cream.

Scratches can be treated with the shoebone as often as you wish.

Rub in the Kiwi wax with a cloth.

The frictional heat caused by the nylon stocking provides a phenomenal gloss.

Put the wax care on the cloth and dab the cloth in water.

The shoebone can also be cleaned.

Wax and water are massaged in layer after layer.

Old cream residues are taken off with the cleaning agent.

Cover the bristles of the polishing brush with a cloth.

The re-greasing effect of the shoebone is achieved by means of the leather oil.

Cover the brush with a nylon stocking.

This way the shoebone can be used for different colors.

Enhanced Care

About every fifth time, shoe care should be done with a mixed emulsion cream (with solvents) for penetrating care and color refreshing. For cordovan shoes, you take an emulsion cream that is especially qualified for horse leather—as it is, for example, available from La Cordonnerie Anglaise.

For shoes with leather soles, the soles can be treated with sole oil every four or five weeks. This is best done with a paint brush. By means of the sole oil, the intake of water during rain is lessened. As a result, the leather becomes firm, abrasion is reduced, and the lifespan is prolonged. In addition, it provides lasting elasticity. By no means should soles come in contact with normal leather oil; the leather would become spongy and the glued areas at the seams would come loose because of the solvents contained in the oil. Because of this, only use solvent-free oil! Prior to using the freshly oiled shoes, they ought to dry at least two days at room temperature, because otherwise there is a danger of slipping, since the soles have become slippery from the oil, or the shoes may produce ugly stains on carpeted floors inside buildings.

Anyone who wears high-quality leather soles tanned with oak bark of the Johannes Rendenbach tannery can abstain from using sole oil altogether. According to Johannes Rendenbach, Jr., owner of the tannery, sole leather tanned in pits with oak bark is already made so water-resistant and robust that a treatment with sole oil would only worsen the quality of the leather.

In case the sole rim and the front of the heel need a color refreshing, edge dye is used. In an emergency, shoe cream can also be used, but the effect is worse and doesn't last for the same amount of time.

Prior to cleaning the shoes, the shoelaces ought to be removed. Firstly, to not smear them with cream or wax, and secondly to care for the shoes in the tying area in an optimal way.

Primary cleaning is done with a horse hair cleaning brush.

The sole rim is dyed with sole dye.

Here you see the difference between dyed and undyed.

Cream is applied with the shoe brush.

Saliva results in more gloss.

Polish with the polishing brush.

Leather soles are treated with sole oil.

Braided Leather Shoes

Such shoes are generally treated the same way as other shoes made from smooth leather. But because of their flexible surface, a soft cloth should be used instead of a hard cleaning brush. The shoe cream is best applied with a finger; this way the cream is able to reach every small nook and cranny. Afterwards polishing is done with a soft goat or yak hair brush.

Spray on the cleaning foam.

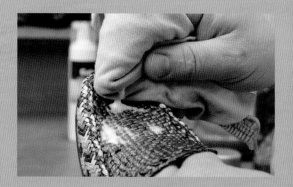

Clean with a soft cloth.

Bama-Waterstop cares and protects.

Solitär also cleans the gaps of braided leather.

Collonil care for braided leather
refreshes the colors.

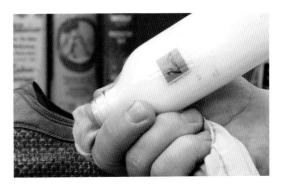

A cloth with care lotion of La Cordonnerie Anglaise.

Woly-Protektor safeguards against dirt.

The care lotion keeps the braided leather flexible.

Patent Leather Shoes

Dirt is removed from them by means of a moist cloth or a very soft brush. Otherwise, there is the danger of damaging the very sensitive varnish layer. Afterwards, they are exclusively treated with care products for patent leather and then polished with a soft cloth or a polishing glove.

Apply Shoeboy's foam for patent leather.

Massage in the patent leather foam.

The Woly Lack Cream is long lasting.

The Bama application sponge is practical.

Pedag varnish cream, too, achieves the best results.

The Pedag cream cleans and cares.

Let the patent leather foam permeate.

Battered patent leather at the shoe's tip ...

... is covered well with nail polish.

Creating Patina

Whoever doesn't want to wait for years and prefers to immediately have a beautiful patina on his/her shoes can create it by alternately applying a shoe cream in accordance with the actual color of the leather, then a darker or brighter one. For light-colored shoes, a darker second dye is applied while for dark shoes a lighter one is used. This can either happen alternately with each shoe care or at once with the lighter dye being applied first, then the darker dye. In general, less of the secondary dye should be used than of the primary dye.

Cover the cloth with the nylon stocking and start polishing.

For the antique finish, apply the light color first.

Take up the darker wax with the shoe brush.

Apply the darker wax to the shoe.

Rub in the wax thoroughly.

Suede Shoes

For shoes made from coarse leather, it is important that they receive a good waterproofing at the very beginning, when the leather is still new. If this is refreshed by later applications of waterproofing, the protective effect will be best.

Cleaning

If salty stains have been created by rain or snow, they can't be simply washed off with water or brushed off. The entire shoe has to be soaked in warm water, best in a big bowl or bucket. A bit of saddle soap can be added to the warm water. Then the shoe is brushed well with a cleaning brush and the so-called salt stains or snow stains, which consist of salt and tanning agents that have become visible on the surface, can be removed. Afterwards, rinse for several minutes under cold, running water and allow to drip dry. For this, the shoe is put with the sole pointing upwards across the water bucket or another receptacle. After about an hour of drying, put in the shoe tree and brush uniformly with a suede leather brush. Afterwards the shoe can be dried in a normal position at room temperature, which takes about twelve to twenty-four hours. If the dried shoe still doesn't meet the needs of the wearer, it can be roughened again by treating it several times with an eraser for coarse leather and the coarse leather brush.

Treat pressure marks with the velour eraser.

Clean the gaps at the upper leather and welt.

Brushes for coarse leather with plastic bristles are gentle to the leather.

Nubuck brushes take up the dirt and smooth the leather.

Water emulsion dyes are environmentally friendly.

Long-handled velour brushes can be well guided.

Apply the cleaning foam to a sponge.

Work carefully with coarse brass brushes.

Cautiously clean the leather by means of the sponge.

All-round plastic velour brush.

Tapir waterproofing spray is only available colorless and with a manual pump.

Care—Suede Shoes

When such shoes are covered with dust, dirty, or look greasy and are brushed with a brass brush (for velour) or a rubber brush (for nubuck), the surface comes clean again. Persistent stains are removed with an eraser for velour. Because of its sandy consistency, the leather usually is slightly ground at the treated area, which causes brighter spots. Then the shoe has to be treated with a color-providing waterproofing agent. If there are no bright spots, a colorless fluid waterproofing product is sufficient, which is either available as spray or, even better, as a fluid waterproofing substance. Afterwards, the shoes are brushed again. During brushing, you always have to take care to only brush in one direction, either with or against the grain;

The wet velour leather finally is brushed to straighten it up. *Photo: Ed. Meier*

only in this way is a uniform look created. The treatment of the leather sole or the sole edges is done as described for shoes of smooth leather.

Fat or oil stains can be treated with a leather shampoo, but most times remain. Bright leather shoes especially, regardless of how pretty they may be, are only fair-weather-shoes.

To remove the stains caused by snow, wet the shoe completely and clean it with saddle soap. *Photo: Ed. Meier*

Photo to the right:
Here the result of the work can be easily recognized. **Important:** Shoes that were completely in the water bath have to be hung up for drying afterwards. To avoid stains created by moisture, stuff the shoes with newsprint. Rumor has it that the *FAZ* [*Frankfurt General Newspaper*] or "*Die Welt*" [*The World*] are better suited than other newspapers because of their smaller black printing ink content.

Foto: Ed. Meier

Two-Tone Shoes

For shoes made of two-toned leather—such as the black and white Spectator models—after cleaning, first the light-colored leather is cared for, then the darker one. In case of much dirt, the work is done with fluid products or a cleaning foam applied with a sponge. In general, shoe cream should be applied very cautiously, which is the reason why brushes with the bristles in line with the handle (pot brushes) or the fingers are best suited for this job. In case a bit of the dark shoe cream ends up on the light-colored leather, it only comes in touch with the bright shoe cream and not with the leather itself. This way it can be removed easier.

Shoes Made of Fabric and Leather

Shoes made from leather and textiles have to be maintained with great care, the textile is usually very sensitive to shoe cream. For the textile part, a separate small cleaning brush should be used. Shoe polish should only be applied with a small pot brush or with fingers. Afterwards, these parts should be polished cautiously and the textile parts ought to be treated with a waterproofing spray. Here, as an exception, an aerosol spray makes sense because with a fluid waterproofing agent the textile parts of the shoes would become thoroughly wet.

Leather Care for Golf Shoes

Only a few shoe types receive as much strain as golf shoes. They have to endure moisture from outside and inside and have to be heat-resistant as well. Heat-resistance is necessary because most golf players put their shoes into the car trunk after the games,

and during summer, the temperatures there easily reach about 176 degrees Fahrenheit [80 degrees Celsius]. Such temperatures dry the leather too rapidly and the upper leather of the shoes get cracks much quicker. This means, don't stow shoes in the car trunk! Golf shoes of smooth leather should be greased well before use. Here, various sports fats are available from Kiwi, Tonino, Burgol Tierowa, Tapir, Colourlock, B & E, Efax, and Centralin, which keep the leather soft and protect it as well. Nowadays, soft spikes are used almost exclusively. If you have to exchange them, you ought to put one drop of oil on the screw thread of metal screw threads when you put in the new spikes. Often there is grass or soil attached to the soles that has to be removed under running water immediately after the game. Then the shoes have to be dried well. Cleaning is best done with a leather cleaner or a cleaning cream. Only after the golf shoes are dry are they treated with a color-providing emulsion cream fitting to the color hue of the upper leather. After a soaking time of about sixty minutes, the golf shoes are polished with a cloth and brush.

It is important that the area at which the upper leather meets the welt is always fatted well. Waxes are not very useful with golf shoes because they don't achieve a high penetrating effect. Don't grease the golf shoes too much, because otherwise the sand of the bunker and loose grass will adhere to the shoes. Rarely do you otherwise go several miles at a stretch, as you do when playing golf, and thus it is important to let the shoes rest with fitting shoe trees for at least forty-eight hours after each wearing. How the various types of upper leather for golf shoes, such as greased leather, white leathers, or combinations of leather and textile, are maintained, you'll read on the following pages.

Sneakers

Sneakers are sports shoes used in everyday life; mostly they look like running shoes or basketball shoes. Meanwhile, there are also sneakers available that combine a classic look with the design of sports shoes. This is the reason why more and more sneakers are worn in the business world. These shoes need a care similar to that of normal street shoes with a few limitations. Because the soles are either made from plastics or rubber, different cleaning agents are required here. The possibilities for combination among sneakers are unlimited, almost as with ladies' shoes. Thus, here are only the most important caring tips. These almost deserve a book of their own.

Nubuck is cleaned with a nubuck rubber brush. The rubber lamellas of the brush smooth the leather.

With textile-leather combinations, apply the cream cautiously with a finger.

Nubuck smooth leather shoes are waterproofed with a multi-purpose spray.

Sneakers of mesh and textile look spick-and-span after cleaning with Hey care.

Textile-leather combinations can be cleaned excellently with Hey.

A waterproofing agent for textile and leather repels water and stains.

Tapir cream is suited well for deep care because of its low viscosity.

The edges of rubber soles last longer with the help of rubber care sprays.

Cleaning Fat-tanned Shoes

The soles are cleaned with a coarse cleaning brush.

Removing the dust by means of a cleaning brush with horsehair bristles.

Applying the cleaning lotion.

Clean the shoelaces as well.

Cleaning the shoes with lotion and a cloth.

Mix Tonino leather cleaner with water.

Cleaning foam is also suited to the task.

Clean the shoes and soles well.

Apply the foam with a soft cloth.

Caring for Fat-tanned Shoes

Threads that stand out are best singed off.

Light-colored seams are protected by neutral fat.

The cream can be applied selectively with fingers.

Apply the cream with the shoe brush.

Disinfection can be done with Kiwi spray for the inside of shoes or ...

The highly-fluid cream of Woly covers very well.

... use Woly Shoefresher, which also provides a better smell to the feet.

Cautiously rub in the cream with a finger.

The edge of the sole is treated neutrally with sole dye.

Polish to a shine with the large horsehair brush.

Finally you waterproof the shoes outdoors.

Caring for Cowboy Boots

Cowboy boots only look really good when they are worn. Thus, it is better to polish them with a cream fitting in color and a darker one to achieve a striking patina.

In order not to stain skirts or trousers with shoe cream, the bootleg ought to be cared for with a care product qualified for textiles. To not change the color of the decorative seams, care for them with a neutral cream.

Cowboy boots only look really good when they are worn. Thus, it is better to polish them with a cream fitting in color and a darker one to achieve a nice patina.

Take up Collonil leather clothing cream with a cloth.

Black wax sticks to the surface very well.

The bootleg is greased with the leather clothing cream.

During the application, rub in more cream in some areas.

For the depth effect ... take cream of a suitable color.

Care for the welt with a shoe brush.

Tonino's shoe trees from cedar wood maintain the stability.

Caring for Hunting Boots

Hunting boots should always be greased well to avoid creaking noises that would startle game animals. Almost every supplier offers leather grease suitable for hunting boots.

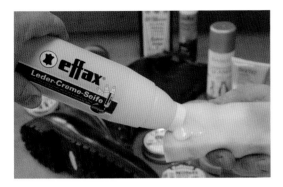

Put Effax leather cleaning cream on a sponge.

Grease the entire boot well, including the rim of the sole.

The Effax cream cleans and cares at the same time.

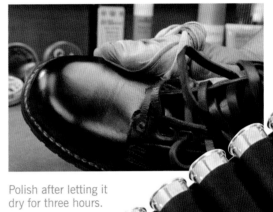

Polish after letting it dry for three hours.

Take up leather grease with the shoe brush.

Ammunition belt of bison leather made by AKAH.

Caring for Hiking Shoes

Remove the coarse dirt with a cleaning brush from horsehair.

Apply the cleaning foam generously.

Rub in the foam by means of a sponge.

Mix it with water according to the instructions.

Fill the Hey cleaner into the dosing cap.

Use the cloth to take up the dirt.

You should close your eyes while applying the Hey cleaning lotion.

Caring for Hiking Shoes

Occasionally you can also waterproof only.

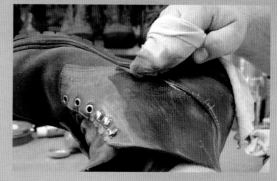

Rub in the leather grease thoroughly.

Put the grease on a soft cloth.

Here you also ought to grease the welt and the rim of the soles.

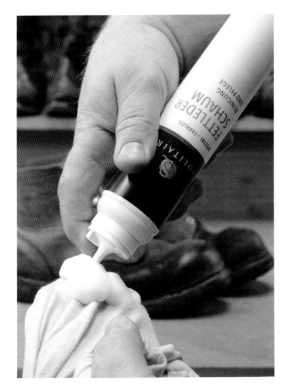

Spray the fat leather foam onto a cloth.

Massage the fat leather foam into the leather thoroughly.

Apply the waterproofing aerosol spray outdoors only.

Keep the rubber flexible by means of Aigle-Care.

Massage the rubber care product into the sole and edge.

Mold has to be treated with Effax.

Caring for Combat Boots

Removing dirt with the cleaning brush.

A toothbrush is helpful in areas that are hard to reach.

Collective shoe care after the mission.

The German armed forces swear by Gregor Chemie.

Old soldier's trick: for better depth effect, light the cream.

Only well-cared-for shoes keep your feet dry.

The cream is distributed well with the shoe brush.

Surplus cream is wiped off.

With the polishing brush and saliva, the shoes are polished to a high gloss.

Caring for Soccer Shoes

To find out about the care of soccer shoes, we watched the equipment keeper of the 1.FC Köln (Cologne), Kresemir Ban, while he was taking care of his shoes. He is effectively the shoe whisperer of the FC. He knows about all the habits and preferences of his players. Some of his tricks we are not allowed to tell, but what you can see here allows your shoes to stay as soft and flexible for a long time as are the shoes of the professionals from the 1.FC Köln.

After each game or training he wet cleans the shoes.

Then the shoes are dried from the inside.

Light and dark brush, leather grease is all he needs.

He applies grease with a polishing brush.

This is no lottery ticket, but his player job card.

In case Cologne wins, he doesn't change his polishing cloth anymore.

He greases the shoes while they are still wet.

After greasing, the shoes dry in rank and file.

For the depth effect, only care with cream.

Oil or grease is sprayed ...

You can rub it in by hand.

... with the Colourlock's fat solvent.

Caring for Racing Shoes

After drying for thirty minutes…

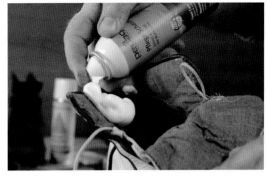

Cleaning foam for the care on the inside.

… the granules are vacuumed off.

The foam can also be used on the outside.

Don't treat the shoes with an aerosol spray.

Nubuck shoes are kept smooth with
the nubuck brush.

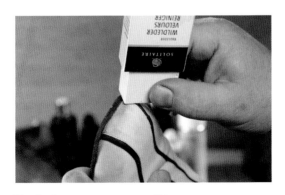

The leather eraser removes dirt.

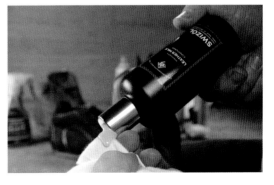

The Swizöl leather cleaner can also be used for shoes.

Caring for Sheepskin Shoes

For the last few winters shoes from lambs fleece have been all the rage. Actually, these boots are not appropriate for bad weather or winter because they are very sensitive to moisture and tend toward stains and bleeding of tanning agents. Always clean the lambs fleece very carefully, and in any case waterproof well.

Here you can see stains from dried tanning agents.

Kiwi leather caring foam works as well.

Clean well with the Hey cleaner.

Rub in the foam with the coarse leather brush.

On the cloth you can see how quickly the leather bleeds out.

Restore the coarse surface.

Treat the wet surface with a brush for coarse leather.

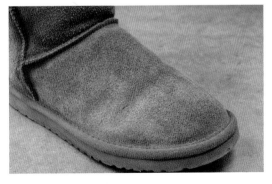

The dried shoe looks like this.

Caring for Exotic Leather Shoes

Exotic leathers, such as snake, salmon, crocodile, ostrich, stingray, or even shark leather, at the moment are very popular. Shoes made of these leather types are always more expensive than those of calf or kid leather. To enjoy them for a long time, there are quite a few things to take into account during care. Care products containing wax are not suitable because they don't provide penetrating greasing. Emulsion creams, lotions, or leather oils are first choice here. By the way, despite all our love for our craft and leather processing, we want to state that exotic leathers that don't originate from animal farms ought to be avoided.

Ostrich leg leather has to be cared for with leather oil.

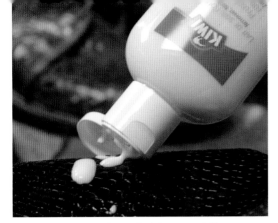

Salmon leather is cleaned with a care lotion.

… or leather oil of Tonino.

Crocodile leather is treated with a leather conditioner.

Woly-cream offers a wide variety of color hues …

Stingray is best cleaned with Woly-foam.

… as only few others do. Here it fits perfectly to the ostrich.

Snake leather likes care lotion as well.

Shark leather is cleaned with a low-viscosity cleaning fluid.

Cayman leather can be well cared for with Tapir …

A low-viscosity emulsion cream of suitable color doesn't change the look.

Caring for White Shoes

White shoes in general only look good in a clean state. White is a symbol for purity and cleanliness. A dirty white shoe appears really scruffy. By the way, white cream has to be applied cautiously because it covers well. All too quickly the soles—or with bicolored shoes, the other color—become white too.

Centralin Shoe White covers well.

In a pinch, Tipp-Ex fluid works as well.

White cream should be applied …

But here it clogs up the holes.

… with the finger, because this way it can be well targeted.

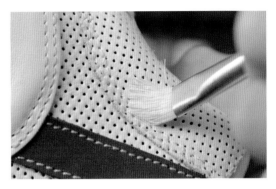

Apply the cream with a paint brush.

Black sole rim color covers maintenance mistakes.

Solitär Deckweiss can be applied easily.

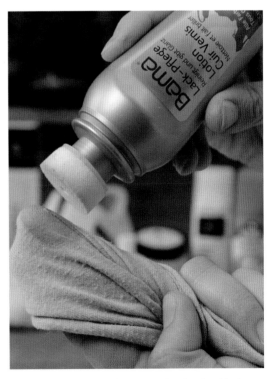

Bama's care product for patent leather is able to gently clean overruns of the white color.

Caring for Women's Shoes

For ladies' shoes the appropriate color hue of the dye is the most important thing.

Nobody else has as many color hues as Woly.

Finally, polish the shoe.

Apply the cream thinly.

Sensitive shoes are treated with Bama waterproofing.

First clean the scratched areas.

Foam shoe trees keep the shape.

Damaged Louboutin soles are a horror.

Dyeing the Ladies' Shoe Soles

The tread sole is ground …

… with a fine abrasive paper.

The dye should be allowed to dry for twenty-four hours.

Apply the appropriate sole dye evenly.

Ladies' Shoes with Embossed Leather

The cleaning bristles also clean gaps.

Polish off the cleaning emulsion with a cloth.

Ladies' shoes are dirty inside from walking barefoot.

The Solitär cleaner can also be used inside the shoe.

The sole can also be cleaned with it.

The rim of the sole is dyed with the sole dye.

Such damage almost physically hurts.

Woly has metallic colors that cover perfectly.

A waterproof marker can be helpful.

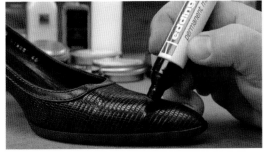

Caring for Ladies' Shoes with Metallic Colors

As you can see, it really works.

Best to wear disposable gloves while applying the dye.

With the shoe brush an ...

With a finger, you can apply the dye with good control.

... emulsion cream is applied and then polished.

As you can see with the latex rubber, the dye adheres well.

Tips for Stain Removal

PIGMENTED SMOOTH LEATHER

Stains on pigmented smooth leather are relatively easy to remove. Since the leather is protected by the layer of pigments, fluids usually roll off and don't penetrate deeply. The fluid is immediately taken off by dabbing with an absorptive cloth or tissue. Don't rub; this only makes things worse. As final step, the stain is treated with a leather cleaner. Spots and lines which were created by pens, especially by ballpoint pens, are removed by first covering them with a masking tape which is then ripped off quickly. The residue is taken up with help of a "dye remover pen" (a special pen for discoloring).

ANILINE LEATHER AND COARSE LEATHER

With these leather types stains permeate quickly and adhere to the leather. For stains from fat or oil a fat-absorbing spray is used; stains which were created by water-containing fluids, such as lemonade, coffee and others, usually demand a complete cleaning with a suitable leather detergent because the stain will become even larger when rubbing or dabbing it with water.

Clothing or leather furniture which has become greasy by contact with skin and sweat have to either be washed completely in the washing machine or be treated with a suitable leather cleaner over the entire area. In both cases the prior use of a color fixer is recommended to avoid a color change. Before washing, a bit of the leather cleaner can already be put on the stained spot directly and be worked by hand; this improves the result.

With coarse leather, a good result is achieved with a coarse leather brush or a leather eraser, as long as you are dealing with dirt from the streets or dust. For streaks from a ballpoint pen you can work with a polishing pad for leather. Be cautious with respect to using masking tape on coarse leather because the fibers may get ripped off.

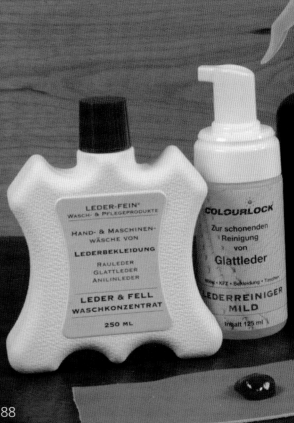

Most Important Rule:

After each stain removal or any cleaning cure, the leather has to be cared for again in order to provide it with fresh nutrients!

The complete removal of grease or wine stains is especially difficult. If you are not sure how to best treat a stain, going to a specialized laundry is not a bad idea!

The Colourlock's fat remover works with all leather types.

Shoe Care Chests and Boxes

For the ignorant among the people caring for shoes it is surely sufficient to stuff the tube of instant gloss into the sock drawer, but by no means is this the case for the pragmatists and aesthetes. Many well-known manufacturers offer small shoe care boxes with the most necessary maintenance tools, as well as large shoe care chests that leave nothing to be desired.

Shoe Care Boxes for the Private Household

Shoe care chests and shoe care boxes for the private household are available in many different sizes and designs. In the upmarket category, you can choose from a series of precious woods and various high-quality content. However, it is important that all tools necessary for regular shoe care be neatly put together in one place and usually in a very decorative way. In any case, the **basic contents** include the following items:

1 can of shoe cream of the most common colors
1 brush for removing dirt
1 shoe brush for each color
1 polishing brush
2 cloths
1 leather cleaner
1 velour brush
1 care product for velour
1 bottle of leather oil
1 neutral cream

(opposite page)
Prince Asfa-Wossen Asserate not only lov
well-tended shoes but also the Royal Sho
Care's cabinet for stowing shoe care tools

Shoe Care Chests for the Private Household

Large shoe care chests are for the shoe care and room decoration aesthetes, since the chests are veritable pieces of furniture, given their respectable size, which can hardly be cleared away or hidden. For this reason, they are usually made of decorative and high-quality woods, such as walnut burl, mahogany, or macassar ebony. If they are well designed, they have a working surface on top and a drawer for dirt. Of course, they also possess a **complete set of shoe care equipment**. To the contents belong:

La Cordonnerie Anglaise most probably has the largest selection.

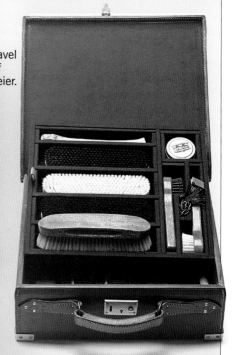

The care product travel suitcase of Eduard Meier.

The Eduard Meier Box has everything you need, even an instruction manual for care.
Photo: Ed. Meier

Foto: Ed. Meier

This small box of La Cordonnerie Anglaise represents the starter-set.

In comparison, this box of La Cordonnerie Anglaise looks more like a noble weapon's case.

With this box of La Cordonnerie Anglaise even a lady turns into a shoe care fanatic.

Shoe Care Chests for the Private Household

Alvoro Design has a clever and very elegant system for stowing shoes with aeration and a panel for storing shoes.

The Dasco care box is equipped by you. It has large brass handles at the sides for easy transport.

Tonino offers various boxes. The one shown is the most adaptable. Be careful, your wife may want to have one of her own!

The box of Alvoro Design also looks very impressive when closed.

Alvoro Design has developed a very handsome and practical care box that is covered with leather and has room for quite a few care products.

The boxes of La Cordonnerie Anglaise are provided with practical leather handles on top.

Shoe Care Service in Hotels

Anyone who has ever seen, even once, shoe polishing machines of the worst kind located even in hotels said to be first-class, or who has witnessed an existing shoe care service completely ruin one's beloved patent leather shoes with common shoe cream of the most disgusting recipe, is able to appreciate genuinely knowledgeable and trained personnel for this work, which is done behind the scenes but is nevertheless important. It is shocking to see what kind of equipment the hotel employees are provided with in many places. Most times, these are the most primitive care products that, including existing brushes and cloths, are all lying together disorderly in a small box that is carried from door to door. The shoes are then tended to by a kneeling employee. That this situation is suboptimal with respect to the motivation of the shoe care personnel and thus doesn't lead to a good result should be clear to everybody. In this case, the hotel could just as well save on the jobs of these employees. Such a "service" can't even be put into the area of pragmatic shoe care anymore.

Hotels that value satisfied guests and want to give their employees a feeling of the value of their work first should invest in good care products and then in the professional training of their personnel. Himer Maßschuhe and Royal Shoe Care offer intensive training sessions to hotels, lasting two days and taking into consideration every shoe care problem. First-class hotels wishing for a care process under optimal conditions ought to consider the purchase of a Royal Shoe Care Station, a large all-inclusive shoe care trolley especially developed for hotels. It is simply rolled from door to door, contains all shoe care means and also has perhaps needed shoelaces for replacement at hand, possesses a robust working surface at a comfortable height, and is also equipped with a drawer for dirt.

A shoe bag for guests of the Carlton Hotel in St. Moritz.

The butler rolls the Royal Shoe Care Station from door to door.

At the Carlton Hotel in St. Moritz, Switzerland, nothing is left to chance with respect to shoe care. All butlers are trained in shoe care during a two-day seminar by Axel Himer. The Royal Shoe Care Station has the right means for every shoe care problem. In Baden-Baden, Germany, the Brenners Parkhotel and Spa cares with the RSC station, too, as does the Sofitel Bayerpost in Munich.

Leather Care Seminars for Superior Caregivers

To the aesthetes among the shoe caregivers, who want to see and learn how shoes are cared for by professionals, we recommend the shoe care seminars of renowned custom shoe makers or professional caregivers. There the participants look into every shoe care problem in an informal atmosphere. Special dates can be set for groups in order to stay among themselves. Such seminars are informative as well as entertaining. Probably the most exclusive shoe care circle is the Swann Club of Olga Berluti in Paris, which is held once a year. Surely not without an ulterior motive, it is named after Marcel Proust's novel character, the Jewish bon vivant Charles Swann. At events of this club, most times in leading five-star hotels, champagne reputedly is not only drunk, but the shoes are polished with it.

If you don't want it as lofty, but nevertheless expect an excellent professional level, you can find it with the shoe care seminars of Shoe Shine Coach, Eduard Meier and Royal Shoe Care. The seminars of the Lederzentrum pass on extensive knowledge about the care and maintenance of leather furniture, automobile leather, and leather wares in general to interested persons.

Peter Meier has led seminars for more than twenty years.

Lederzentrum trains for automobile leather and furniture care, as well as the subject of smart repair.

Rainer Ersfeld also trains shoe care enthusiasts.

Axel Himer transfers his maintenance expertise to professionals and ordinary persons.

Implementing the lessons learned gives confidence when dealing with the care products.

Common care is communicative as well. Seminars for professionals last from four hours up to two days.

Shoe aficionado Mick Knauff of *Deutsches Anleger Fernsehen* [*German Investors TV*] during the care seminar of Saphir importer Torsten Dickmann.

Shoes for Travel

Anyone who wants to treat their shoes in a way that best keeps their value while traveling doesn't get around some basic considerations. First of all, you should always use shoe trees; light travel shoe trees are sufficient. If you don't want to carry around too many shoe trees, use one pair for the most recently worn shoes and stuff the other shoes with newsprint.

For transport, breathable shoe bags are recommended; in no case use airtight plastic bags. A travel shoe care set, such as offered by many companies, should also be carried along each time you're traveling. Depending on the length of the trip, it should be filled with:

1 can of shoe cream of the most important color
2 shoe brushes (the best are small pot brushes)
1 small polishing brush
1 cloth
1 travel shoehorn
1 brush for coarse leather

Foto: Ed. Meier

Foto: Ed. Meier

Eduard Meier offers handsome leather travel sets that are supplied with the absolutely necessary items. *Photo: Ed. Meier*

La Cordonnerie Anglaise offers a wide variety of travel sets; we couldn't show all of them.

Shoes ought to be filled with a foldable or plastic shoe tree (because of the weight). Letting shoes travel inside a shoe bag protects clothing. A travel set with the most necessary care products and replacement shoelaces should also always be on board.

Shoeshine Professionals from Berlin to LosAngeles

INTRODUCTION

Shoeshine professionals were a common sight in Germany until about 1940. Then they were hit by the same fate as, for example, attendants at gas stations, porters, and many others who offered their services in public and whose jobs by and by vanished from the public eye. In my opinion, social envy and "stealthy socialism," which appeared in Germany starting at the end of World War II, are the reason that today it is no longer respectable to be publicly serviced. Anyone who nevertheless dares to sit down in the chair of one of the few shoeshine professionals who can be seen again of late can be sure of the derisive looks of his/her fellow human beings. Because with this action, he/she assures that he/she belongs to the world of high finance, which exploits the working class until there is nothing left.

With respect to gas station attendants, I can only say that with today's gas prices not only service but coffee and a meal, too, should be included in the price.

Anyone using the services of a porter, of course, is naturally seen as a lazy and slothful person because anybody who has two arms should carry the baggage himself/herself. Unless the person in question is senior or disabled—but woe to the porter who dares to ask them for money. Here, of course, manners demand that their baggage is carried out of kindness. Many taxi drivers naturally don't see themselves as porters, either, which is why, at best, they open the trunk for their customer so he/she can stow baggage themselves. If the drivers do it themselves, they in turn expect an especially generous tip for this "extraordinary" service. The social progress in this is not really obvious for a reasonable thinking human being. The almost complete disappearance of such services contributed decisively to the often-quoted "service desert Germany." There is absolutely nothing disreputable about using such services—but to walk around with dirty shoes is indeed an insult to your fellow human beings. The social stigma that hits these professions should rather be used on bank managers. After all, nobody has a problem with letting the mail be delivered to their homes, although they could also take it home from the post office themselves, or with receiving meals and service in restaurants although they could cook at home as well. When thinking of the friendliness of the waiters, this seems to be an attitude that must have been especially wide-spread in the former GDR. You should only be ashamed of using such services if you are not willing to pay for them in a proper way, because these are all honest jobs that, done well, also need to be rewarded.

POST NO BILLS

VIOLATORS
WILL BE
PROSECUTED

Shoeshine professional Peter Wiggins,
Shoe Shine Downtown, Los Angeles.

Shoeshine Professionals from Berlin to Los Angeles

Not a few successful careers have started with a job as shoeshine professional and doing this job never harmed anyone As examples, we mention the multi-million dollar diamond dealer Ludwig Nissen, who in nineteenth century New York brushed shoes as a German emigrant, the former heavy-weight boxer and world-champion Larry Holmes as well as Luiz Inácio da Silva, who even achieved presidency of his native country Brazil.

The eleven-year-old Ethiopian shoeshine professional Tutobo Repigo brings this discrepancy to a point very well. "My people most times don't see the value of my work. Because of this, most look down on us shoeshine boys. But especially the shoeshine professionals need your respect."

Of course, the situation in countries with child labor is very different. Nevertheless, we want to reassure our readers here that the authors, who as Kim and Alex Himer, Cologne, naturally clean and polish many shoes and were also at many fairs and events featuring shoe care professionals with their booths,

"Kaiser" Franz Beckenbauer used the Royal Shoe Care Chair for his charity golf tournaments.

at no time had the impression of doing an inferior or even superfluous work. And with a daily income of more than $390 [300 euros], we can't talk about a dead end with respect to the job either.

Having said this, we hope that the service of shoeshine professionals and other service providers will be used again increasingly. In the following, we introduce some typical and not-so-typical representatives of this career field.

On German TV, Sonya Kraus had her sandal straps cared for with gold.

ZDF news anchorman Claus Kleber values good service.

For the *SWR* program "Kaffee oder Tee" ["Coffee or Tea"] Axel Himer was invited as a professional consultant with respect to shoe care and answered the viewers' questions on this topic.

Shoeshine Event— Nitschmann

Jürgen Nitschmann has been performing his job as a shoeshine professional since 1995 at fairs and in the entertainment area. He doesn't see himself as an absolute professional, but as the interface between the employer and his customers. But this doesn't mean that his shoe care is bad with respect to work and result. He tells that once a man had his shoes cleaned at a fair and was so enthusiastic about the result that he asked whether he would be allowed to bring the rest of his shoes to have them cleaned as well. After he was told that this wouldn't be a problem, he brought twelve pairs of shoes to the booth, believe it or not.

Set-up, decorations, and costumes are in an authentic 1920s-style and special emphasis is put on a very friendly and courteous customer treatment.

The Shoeshine Event—Nitschmann can be booked for all events in Germany and worldwide.

www.der-schuhputzer.de

The Nitschmann team cares for the customers' shoes not only very well but also very stylishly.

SPS Shoe Care Service

Thomas Ganick has been a "shoeshine professional out of Berlin and passion" since 2004. Back then, he was without a job and didn't want to work in his old profession again. From the $2,500 [2,000 euros] he received for participating in a medical study he bought his first shoe care equipment. None of the different jobs he had done before during his lifetime had satisfied him as much as this. He explains it as, on the one hand, always being in intensive contact with interesting people and on the other, as immediately seeing the result of his work and receiving positive response to it. After all, the satisfaction of his customers is uppermost on his agenda. The Shoe Care Service can be booked for all kinds of events, as long as the quality of the work is an important factor to the host. A pleasant and entertaining conversation then comes up naturally.

Thomas Ganick is a passionate shoeshine professional.

In Ethiopia, shoeshine professional is a job for survival.

Besides the shoe care at a given location, a pick-up and delivery service for companies and private persons is offered as well. Care delivery all across Germany and shoe repairs done by a master shoemaker complete the services on offer.

www.mein-schuhputzer.de

Listros e.V.

A special project is Listros e.V., a charitable society in Berlin founded in 2003 by the Ethiopian Dawit Shanko. The goal of the society is to improve the lives of children and adolescents who work as shoeshine professionals in Ethiopia and are called "*listros*" there. With the support of Kiwi and other companies, 3,500 shoe care boxes were brought to Germany and exhibited there. In return, the children were enabled to build new shoe care boxes under the tutelage of carpenters with the materials provided. The old ones can be bought at a price of $3,200 [2,500 euros]. Fifty percent of the sales revenue goes as starting capital to the Listros Bank in Ethiopia, the other fifty percent is used by the society for events and exhibitions. The exhibition "*Perspektivwechsel*" (Changing Perspective) was opened by German president Christian Wulff at October 26, 2010. www.listros.de

German president Christian Wulff together with the founder of Listros e.V., Dawit Shanko.

A *listro* with his new Kiwi care box.

German president Christian Wulff opened the exhibition "Perspektivwechsel" ["Change of Perspective"] of Listros e.V. at the Arkaden am Potsdamer Platz [Arcades at Potsdamer Platz] in Berlin on October 26, 2010.

Riding Equipment Care

Introduction

Horses have been kept as farm and production animals for millennia, and for centuries they have served as entertainment, for example, at various tournaments of equestrian sports and for leisure time activities. The nomadic peoples of central Asia, the ancient Celts, the Romans, and Greeks all used horses for agriculture, transport, and the military. The vast empire of Genghis Khan was conquered on horseback and Alexander the Great named an entire city after his horse Bucephalus, which had carried him from Macedonia to India. The Roman emperor Caligula's nickname "Little Boot" derived from the soldier's boots he already wore as an adolescent. During his lifetime he was never called by this name; this would have been lethal for anyone who dared. Not only did he construct a marble palace for his favorite horse Incitatus ["Hotspur"], but he also wanted to appoint it consul.

The breed of the noble Arab horses reputedly traces back to the five mares Hamdaniyah, Hadbah, Abayyah, Saqlawiyah, and Kuhaylah, which distinguished themselves by exceptional loyalty towards the prophet Muhammad and were blessed by him. A descendant of these mares, the stallion Darley Arabian, which came to England in 1705, is seen as the progenitor of the English thoroughbreds.

On June 18, 1815, at the battle of Waterloo, not only 47,000 humans were killed, but countless horses as well, among them the battle horse of Napoleon Bonaparte, a white horse named Marengo. The British commanding officer, Arthur Wellesley, Duke of Wellington, brought it as a trophy to London, where its bones reputedly are still shown on display in a museum. Towards his own battle horse, the mare "Copenhagen," which died in 1836, Wellington was much more respectful. He had it buried with all military honors. But the Prussians, who had stood on the side of the United Kingdom under the supreme command of field marshal Gebhard Leberecht Fürst Blücher von Wahlstatt (the shoe model "Blücher von Wahlstatt" was named after him), had to endure losses among their battle horses, too. For example, two battle horses of Blücher's chief of staff, field marshal August Graf Neidhardt von Gneisenau, were shot during the battle.

Probably the best known racehorse is "Man o' War," 1917–1947, was awarded "racehorse of the century" in 1999. During his career "Man o' War" won twenty out of twenty-one races and won $249,465 of trophy money—at a time at which a Model T Ford cost no more than $400. The American racehorse "Seabiscuit" achieved great fame during the 1930s and, among others, raced against "War Admiral," a descendant of Man o' War. In 2003, Hollywood set a monument for Seabiscuit in making a movie about him.

One of the most famous German racehorses is "Oleander," which up to now is the only one, next to the mare "Kinscem," that could win the Grand Prize of Baden three times from 1927 to 1929. In his honor, the venerable Brenner's Park Hotel in Baden-Baden named its bar "Oleander Bar." Whoever consumes a drink there will see a painting of the famous chestnut stallion on the wall.

As a movie horse, "Beauty" (original name "Highland Dale") has achieved unsurpassed fame. It played the main part in *The Adventures of Black Beauty*, *Fury,* and in *Giant* next to Elizabeth Taylor and James Dean.

Uwe Töns, polo captain of Team Epona
and his horse Mimosa distinctly show what
harness and saddle have to endure.

Some Native American tribes of North America buried high-ranking persons, especially chiefs, sitting on their dead horses.

We can say without exaggeration that keeping horses as production animals sped up the progress of civilization decisively and enriched it considerably. In many countries of the third world, horses are still indispensable work forces in agriculture and essential as mounts and draft animals. Argentina's gauchos and American cowboys are only able to guide and supervise the giant cattle herds with help from their horses. Even the modern armies of Switzerland and Austria, as well as a small subdivision of the German mountain infantry, still have horses used as pack animals on forbidding mountain paths.

If you consider that, with a worldwide population of more than sixty million horses, more than a million horses and ponies are living in Germany, in addition to almost two million riders and even more fans of equestrian sport, it becomes obvious that equestrian sport and the entire "horse department" from fan to breeder still has a

respectable rank in our society. This can also be seen by the almost unlimited number of equipment items that are mostly made from leather.

Saddles

Saddles exist in almost unlimited numbers. They are available as dressage saddles, show jumping saddles, versatility saddles, Western saddles, military saddles, jockey saddles, sidesaddles, and packsaddles. Anyone who owns especially precious, custom-made saddles won't shy away from even the most intensive care effort.

Saddles inevitably are subjected to high mechanical loads and, during rides, come in contact with rain and horse sweat, which attack the protecting fat layer of the leather time and again and even destroy it. Thus for regular care, re-greasing saddle soap is indeed best. It contains cleaning, caring, and re-greasing substances. Saddle soap is applied to the leather with a moist sponge in circular movements. It is especially important to clean the underside of the saddle and the harness, too, which is in direct contact with the horse's skin. For even more rigorous care, after cleaning, the dry saddle is treated with leather balm or leather oil, which is also applied with a sponge or a cloth.

In principle, leather grease can also be used, but, because of the strong re-greasing effect, here you have to take care that surplus grease is wiped off with a clean cloth prior to the next use. Otherwise, it can happen that the grease is transferred onto your clothing.

The Argentinean Eduardo Romero is groom as well as polo player at Epona and gave us valuable care tips.

June 17, 1956, during the Olympic Games at Stockholm: Hans Günter Winkler on Halla in the show jumping course.

This is the original Olympic saddle, which was made for the multiple Olympic winner Hans-Günter Winkler by the company Waldhausen of Cologne. A saddle series was modeled after it. The saddle is on display at Waldhausen's own museum.

Two-Tone Saddle

The practical box for horse care products has to be filled by you.

Spray the leather well with the leather cleaner.

Centralin Shoe White is a remedy here.

Rub in the cleaner well.

Put the white dye on a neutral base ...

For lazy people, there is a combination of detergents and care products available.

... take it up with a fine paint brush ...

Sooner or later the white inlay becomes shabby.

... and distribute it carefully. Let dry for twenty-four hours.

Saddle Cleaning

Saddle cleaning is often neglected; most times the riders use saddle soap for everything. But meanwhile very good, modern means exist, which also have their special justification and lead to best results. In any case, cleaning dirt and sweat is also an important part of care and should always be done thoroughly.

Apply the Lexol cleaner to a sponge ...

... and dry it with the cloth.

... then massage it well into the leather.

Saddle soap is available as bars or in pots.

Clean with a soft cloth and rub the saddle dry.

The soap has a cleaning and re-greasing effect.

The cleaner can also be applied directly
and left to work for a while.

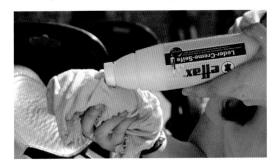

The Effax care cream is well-suited for travel.

Then use pressure to rub it in with a sponge ...

It cleans and cares without having to use water.

Bridles and Reins

Bridles and reins basically have to be cleaned and cared for in the same way as saddles. But since they are difficult to treat because of their small width, it is recommended to mix soap suds of saddle soap and water in a bucket and to clean the harness under water speedily with a sponge. Afterwards, it has to be dried thoroughly at room temperature (or inside the stable), best done overnight. Don't use artificial heat sources! Finally apply some caring agent (leather oil, leather balm, or leather grease) on a cloth, clasp reins or harness with it, and draw them through the cloth. It is best not to use any leather grease for the reins because it doesn't penetrate deeply and the reins may become slippery. Besides that, some reins are made from coarse

Waldhausen's textile bag for care products is not only spacious enough for stowing all kinds of cleaning and caring equipment but, as you can see, it can also be hung up by its carrying strap in a practical way.

The harness can be …

… cleaned very well with the Hey cleaner.

Textiles can also be …

… cleaned with it in a gentle way.

Saddle

For the care of saddles a multitude of oils, fats, emulsions and waterproofing sprays exist, which often end up unused. As mentioned before, this happens because many riders believe that saddle soap is sufficient for the care. But this is not the case. Especially in equestrian sport, the saddle is stressed very much by sweat and abrasion. With respect to the costs of a new leather saddle, caring for it really makes sense.

B & E leather oils are available in black and neutral colors.

... then rub it in with circular movements.

For dark saddles you can use the black oil.

Leather balm is well-suited for intermediate care.

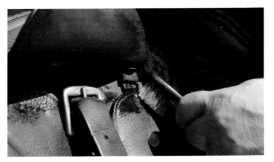

Invisible areas have also to be cared for.

Polish the saddle with the polishing brush.

After sixty minutes of drying, rub off the saddle.

To protect the saddle from dirt, it can also be waterproofed prior to storage.

Soak a soft cloth with caring oil ...

Polo Players— Equipment

Polo equipment is very large and a bit problematic with respect to care, because by tradition white is the preferred color. A polo player looks like a modern gladiator on horseback. Maintenance is usually done by a separately employed caretaker who also cares for the horses. Usually these are Argentineans because they grow up with polo sports in the way we Germans grow up with soccer. These important people working in the background are called grooms. But, as already mentioned before, they love to use saddle soap. Thus, it is about time that grooms learn about the fantastic possibilities of modern leather care. Meanwhile there exist attempts to make polo accessible to a broader audience without having to own eight horses. Nevertheless, it probably won't become a popular sport, seen that show jumping is a real bargain compared to it.

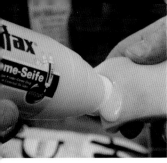

ply Effax cream soap to a sponge ...

Erdal White covers very well.

and clean the helmet.

With the bar of saddle soap ...

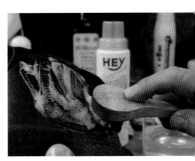

The Hey product is applied with the shoe brush.

e Hey cleaner can also be used.

... the knee protectors' outsides can be perfectly cleaned.

Apply Bama grease to the outside of the protectors.

ong dirt is removed especially well.

Saddle soap delivered in pots is also well suited.

Then massage in with the shoe brush.

rowa leather detergent
ans and cares.

B & E also delivers the sponge with the pot.

225

It is important that the rubbed-in fats are also allowed to come in contact with textiles.

Riding Boots

Remove dust with the cleaning brush.

Basic cleaning is done either with the Hey cleaner and brush …

… or with the leather cleaner of Eduard …

The polo boots are thoroughly polished.

… Meier, which is applied with a sponge.

The area of the welt has to be cleaned thoroughly, too.

Rub the boots clean with a cloth.

Polish the cream or wax with a cloth.

You can also use the cream soap by Effax.

Clean the sole with a coarse brush.

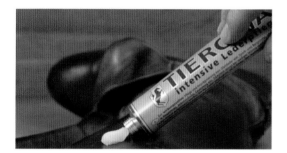

Apply the Tierowa leather grease for deep care.

Let the sole oil sink into the leather sole.

Apply wax for the gloss.

Clean the polo gloves with Hey.

Don't forget the welt.

The positive result is clearly visible here.

Riding Boots

The Hey cleaner is poured in the dosing cap …

… and mixed with water. Then …

... the sole is cleaned with the cleaning brush.

Take emulsion cream out of the pot ...

Rub the sole dry with a cloth.

... and apply thinly.

Apply Effax cream soap to a cloth ...

Take up wax with the shoe brush.

... and clean the boots intensely.

Finally, the boot is polished to a high gloss.

Leather Clothing Care

INTRODUCTION

Thanks to its outstanding qualities, such as durability, breathability while being tight against the wind, as well as abrasion hardness, leather is often made into clothing. For many indigenous peoples, leather was and still is the only material for the production of skirts, trousers, and jackets. Rough life conditions and extreme climatic conditions most times don't allow the use of textiles because these are too sensitive. In modern society as well, leather clothing is not only used as workwear, but also as elegant leisure wear. Traditional costumes are even worn at festive occasions, just think of the Bavarian Lederhosen. Even fine leather clothing is in general very tough and doesn't need much care. By wearing it, the leather stays soft and flexible and even occasional contact with rainwater usually doesn't do any damage.

Cleaning and Washing in General

Very dirty or greasy-looking leather clothing, regardless of whether it is smooth leather, coarse leather or aniline leather, in general can be cleaned with leather detergent. As an alternative, detergent for woolen fabrics or fluid, and neutral soap can be used. Rather sensitive and slightly dirty leather such as nappa is better washed manually; more robust and dirtier leather clothing such as motorcycle outfits can also be washed in the machine at 86° Fahrenheit [30° Celsius] with the program for woolen fabrics. For washing manually, several rounds of washing are recommended in order to clean the pieces of clothing thoroughly. With pieces of different colors or clothing made from a mixture of leather and textiles, staining or color bleeding can occur. Here a color fixer for leather ought to be used, which largely prevents the bleeding of dyes and tanning agents. In general, only pieces of the same color should be washed together and with sets always all pieces at the same time, because otherwise differences in color may occur. Please, pay attention to the instructions of each care product. The process of drying can be sped up by wrapping a cloth around the wet leather clothing and pressing the water out of the leather; do not wring it out. Afterwards, the clothing is hung on the laundry rack and dried at room temperature; don't hang it on top of a heater or in direct sunlight. After three to four days, approximately, the leather clothing is completely dry again but somewhat stiff, an effect that diminishes quickly after wearing the piece again. The dry leather then should be waterproofed thoroughly. The waterproofing agent shouldn't contain any silicone because this gums up the pores and thus impairs the breathability of the leather. Pieces of clothing that possess breathable membranes under the leather surface in general are washed the same way. However, there are special washing detergents available, which are only suitable for this mixture of leather and textile.

Although coarse leather clothing is more sensitive than clothing of smooth leather, it is cleaned the same way. Because of the easy creation of water stains if the clothing is only cleaned partly, it is recommended to always moisten the entire piece when washing manually. The leather fibers of the dry leather, which have been squeezed flat, are erected again by means of a crepe brush (for nubuck leather) or a brass brush (for velour leather). Afterwards, waterproof thoroughly.

Deer leather clothing of the company Hack Lederwaren in Cologne, Germany.

Suede

For suede there are special dyeing agents available—don't use dyes for smooth leather. These special dyes are used in accordance with the product's instructions. First test the color hue at an inconspicuous spot. Afterwards, it is recommended to waterproof the leather anew and to roughen it by means of a brush for coarse leather. Greasy-looking spots can be roughened by means of the coarse leather brush and stains can be removed with the coarse leather eraser. About two times a year the piece of clothing should be treated with a fluid waterproofing agent for coarse leather.

Spray the Woly-Cleaner and …

Be careful with the eraser with chamois-tanned deer leather!

… massage in carefully with the brush.

Clean the deer leather cautiously with the velour brush.

Every once in a while the deer leather clothing should be waterproofed.

Spray stains with the cleaning foam …

Stains can also be removed with Colourlock.

… and rub it in with the brush.

Important! Don't rub, only dab!

Smooth Leather

Pigmented Smooth Leather Clothing

Pigmented smooth leathers are treated with leather oil twice a year—it cares for and waterproofs the leather. If color refreshing is needed, a color refresher can be used for fine leather clothing, but the leather has to be de-greased before by means of petroleum ether. If you are not sure about how to do the color refreshing, you had better go to specialty companies for help. For rather coarse motorcycle outfits and workwear, black leather oil can be used. As usual, it is also valid here that you had better test the product first at an inconspicuous spot. For cleaning, a leather detergent is applied with a sponge.

Aniline Leather

For aniline leather, special care products are available, which make it insensitive to water. Special aniline protectors with protection against UV prevent the leather from bleaching and are re-greasing. These aniline protectors should be applied twice a year. Since aniline leather is a leather type with open pores, it is very sensitive to water and other fluids. Thus, it is especially important to waterproof this leather thoroughly immediately after purchase.

Color Refreshing

When the leather has become discolored or has large scratches, color refreshing may be necessary. At first the leather is cleaned with a leather detergent and afterwards de-greased with petroleum ether. Then the leather dye for smooth leather is applied. Here it makes sense to first test at an inconspicuous spot whether the color hue is correct. Please, stick to the instruction manual. Afterwards, the leather is treated with leather oil or care lotion.

Caring for the smooth horse leather jacket with Kiwi.

Collonil Black is well suited for the care of dark items.

For quick care in between use a caring cloth.

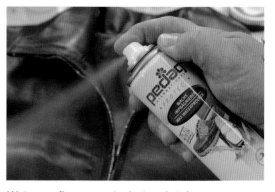

Waterproofing prevents dust and stains.

Solch ein Fettfleck auf der Weste ist wohl der Supergau.

A greasy stain like this on the vest is most probably the worst case scenario.

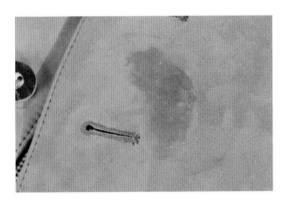

Don't treat this stain with household remedies.

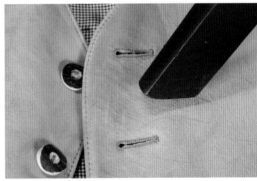

Vacuum after letting dry for thirty minutes.

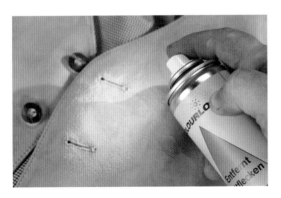

Spray on the Colourlock stain remover.

Roughen with a fine velour brush.

Grease Stain Removal

Symbols for Leather Care

Many leather products have labels or embossings with symbols and instructions for care. The exact meaning of these symbols is listed here:

Leather Skin

The symbol for real leather per se, usually combined with the description "Genuine Leather" ["*Echtes Leder*"]. But what is the meaning of this?

In the RAL agreement 060 A2 of the RAL German Institute for Quality Assurance and Certification e.V., which is virtually German law, "real leather" is described as follows:

"As leather, real leather, or any expression which in common opinion refers to leather or a leather type (such as boxcalf, nappa, nubuck, saffian, and so on) for offer and sale only a material can be named as such, which is produced from split or unsplit animal skin or the fur by means of tanning and while keeping the structure of grown fibers in their natural braided state."

For leather with a cover layer from plastics, for example, the layer is not allowed to be thicker than 0.15 mm. For a more intense finish or a thicker layer the naming directives for "*Leder mit Beschichtung*" [leather with surface coating] apply.

Leather Clothing

The care labels for textiles are partly taken over for leather clothing as well. The symbols are standardized and protected by law. The care labels mention the maximum possible treatment; more gentle treatments are possible anytime. For the sake of completeness, for each care method a statement has to

be made. The order of these statements is dictated as follows:

Washing

This symbol gives information about whether the piece of clothing can be

washed at all, regardless of whether this is done manually or in the washing machine. Possibly stated numbers give the maximum washing temperature. If the washing trough is underlined once, a gentle treatment has to be chosen; this means using the delicate wash cycle for machines. If the trough is underlined twice, an especially gentle treatment has to be used; this means the cycle for woolen textiles of the washing machine. If there is a hand depicted in the trough, only manual washing is allowed. If the symbol is crossed, washing is not allowed at all.

With leather, you have to take care that only special leather detergents are used in accordance with the instructions.

Bleaching

The empty triangle shows that peroxide-

based bleaches as well as chlorine-based bleaches can be used. Two tilted lines mean that no chlorine-based bleach, only peroxide bleaches are allowed. A crossed triangle prohibits any bleach. For leather, this symbol is always crossed because leather in principle should not be bleached. After all, the color should be conserved.

Drying

The square symbolizes the drying process; a circle inside the square stands for

a tumble dryer. Thus with this symbol drying with the tumble dryer is allowed; the same is valid, if there are two dots inside the circle. With only one dot, drying is only allowed at low temperatures. If the symbol is crossed, no drying by mechanical means is allowed. This is valid for about all leather types because leather should exclusively be dried at room temperature, for otherwise it can shrink and shrivel.

Ironing

The iron shows whether a piece of clothing can be ironed or not.

The presence of dots show the temperature range: three dots represent hot, two dots medium, and one dot means low temperature without steam. If the symbol is crossed, no ironing is allowed. Leather should only be ironed in exceptional cases, when dry at a maximum of 113 degrees Fahrenheit [45 degrees Celsius] and never be steamed. Also, a heat-resistant membrane should always be put between leather and iron; baking parchment is best suited.

Professional, chemical cleaning

The circle shows whether professional, chemical cleaning can be done. Displayed letters inside the circle indicate the chemicals that can be used for the cleaning process.

If the symbol is underlined, the meaning is the same as with the "washing" icon. A crossed circle states that no chemical cleaning is allowed. For high-quality leather clothing, it is recommended to go to a professional dry-cleaner's right away, in case this is allowed by the manufacturer.

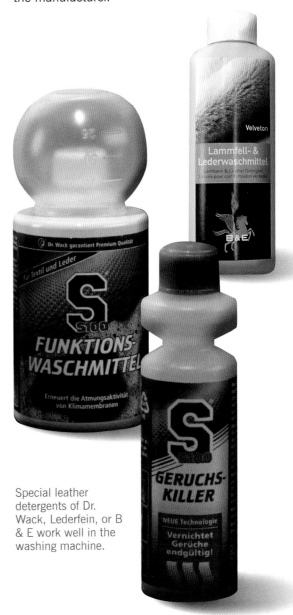

Special leather detergents of Dr. Wack, Lederfein, or B & E work well in the washing machine.

Motorcycle Outfits

Motorcycle outfits by nature are very robust and are usually made from cow leather, rarely from kangaroo leather. Through dead insects, engine heat, and contact with metal, they are more stressed and battered than any other leather clothing. After all, they are meant to absorb falls that hopefully never occur and to give maximum protection to the driver.

In general, motorcycle outfits can be washed or cleaned in the same way as described earlier. Very dirty spots or stains caused by dead insects ought to be pretreated manually with leather detergent and a brush. Some leather detergents can also be used with a leather-textile-mixture; here you should follow the instruction manual in any case. After drying at room temperature, a leather care lotion or oil is applied to waterproof and maintain.

Caution:
Never use shoe polish for the care of leather textiles!!!

Motorcycle Leather

Textile-leather combinations can be maintained well with Dr. Wack.

Thinly apply the Dr. Wack waterproofing spray.

Apply the Hey cleaner with a brush.

Lexol's conditioner has UV-protection.

Rub clean with a soft cloth.

The Woly waterproofing also has a good effect.

Hey's fluid care product can also be used on plastics.

Cleaning with the saddle soap works as well.

… and massage it in well.

For the helmet, the Woly cleaner …

The Grison leather soap can be used, too.

… that even takes up salts is well-suited.

Roughen the palm of the gloves …

Put Tierowa leather cleaner on the cloth …

… and waterproof with Dr. Wack Rau-Matt Pflege [Rough-Matte Care].

Motorcycle Boots

Motorcycle boots have to protect the foot and leg during a fall, have to be waterproof, and, of course, have to conform to the rest of the outfit. Here we show how to care for modern racing boots and fat-tanned boots from calf leather.

Spray the boots with Shoeboy's cleaning foam.

Massage in the foam with a cloth.

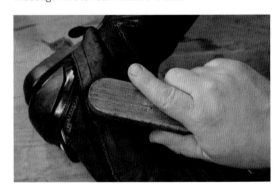

Remove dust with the coarse leather brush.

Clean velour with the brush.

Collonil clothing fat can also ...

Treat the velour part with a spray for coarse leather.

... be used for the care of boots.

Low-viscosity leather cream of Tierowa ...

Polish leather cream with a soft cloth.

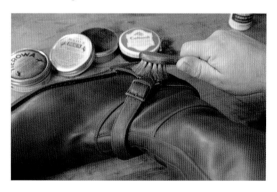

... is applied with the shoe brush.

Finally apply a waterproofing spray.

Polish with the horse hair polishing brush.

Leather Bag and Suitcase Care

Introduction

Bags and suitcases in general have to endure much. Here it doesn't matter whether it is a favorite handbag, a briefcase, or a travel suitcase. Especially travel baggage today is handled roughly and without respect by their owners as well as the ground personnel at the airport. You get the impression that as soon as something is stowed for travel, it is only worth half the money.

In former times, this was totally different—and in this case indeed better. For only wealthy people could afford to travel to some summer resort and, of course, all the beloved "necessities" from home ought to be with them. Not only was the complete wardrobe for all kinds of weather and social occasions, but also some of the dishes and the furniture, were taken on a trip. After all, nothing should be lacking. Of course, the precious porcelain, the custom-made suits, handmade hats and top-hats, and the welt-sewn shoes were especially well protected. Each piece had to have enough space during travel. Nothing was crammed or stuffed in. This attitude led to the development of spacious and stable travel baggage, which found its culmination in the wardrobe trunk, which needed to be handled by two men even when it was empty. Quite often for car trips, a separate luggage car was added, which was steered by the chauffeur who followed the car of the nobility. Besides wood, back then as well as today, wear-resistant leather was valued as preferred material for such luggage. Of course, it is easy to understand that nowadays only the British Queen can afford such travel style. By the way, it is known that, among other things, her own mattress is part of the equipment taken on travel by Her Majesty. With respect to the beds of some hotels, this is something that is surely wished for by many travelers. Nevertheless, despite today's travel customs and the wardrobe that is really not that precious anymore for many people, there is no reason to treat the content in the aforementioned manner.

The fact that the favorite handbag of a lady or the daily-used briefcase of a manager suffer in similar ways over the years and quite often have to endure scratches should not surprise anybody either. All the more important is good care.

The adventures a leather bag can experience are made clear in the poem "The Bag" by Jürgen Daube:

The Bag

This bag, as some of you may know,
was recently made, though the leather is old.
But good leather—and every child knows this—
is made from cattle, a fact not to miss.

For many years, you might have seen,
on top of a vaulting box it had been.
And every pupil had to succeed
to jump over the vaulting box indeed.
This way the leather over many years
learned much of courage and of fears.

And if you listen carefully
it still speaks of the cow and the pupils to thee.

And at some point, some specific event
a hole occurred. Or was it a dent?
The leather's time at the top was over,
but—thanks to Jürgen—it could start all over.

And since only a small part looked like a mess
I went and collected all of it, yes,
which according to my own design
I sewed together to make a bag this fine.

If you happen to own such a specific bag
there is no doubt, it has "unique" on its tag.
Each of the bags, you can be sure,
has such a unique history as yours.

The bag's uniqueness has many reasons:
the leather bears traces of many seasons,
the natural tanning, the color, too,
not to forget the design, which pleases you.

Recycling's in vogue, and thus the leather
received a third life when I sewed it together.
I hope you'll have fun with wearing the bag
and will frequently do so—I'd enjoy that.

P.S.
For the last third of the leather's life I recommend
using translucent polish every now and then.
For touching-up, I also give advice,
it's good to use leather grease sometimes.

Cleaning and Care of Leather Bags and Suitcases

For stains and dirt, a leather detergent is used, and for care and waterproofing, depending on the intensity of use, leather oil is used about twice a year. Especially with larger luggage pieces, which are subjected to more stress, a thin layer of leather grease can be applied with a cloth. But because of its re-greasing effect, the leather grease should only be applied on the outside.

Bags and suitcases of aniline leather are treated with special care products for aniline that have maintaining and waterproofing effects at the same time. For cleaning, special aniline detergents are at your disposal; oil or fatty stains are removed by means of a fat-absorbing spray.

Use only gentle care products for the maintenance of suitcases. Saddle soap is not suited for fine leathers.

These gray surfaces were caused by saddle soap.

Kiwi offers an all-round care product.

Put Colourlock foam cleaner on a sponge.

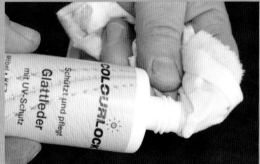

The Colourlock smooth leather care also offers UV-protection.

Ed. Meier's detergent cleans well and gently.

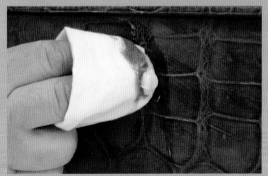

You achieve best results with the Colourlock care dye.

Suede

In case they are very dirty or heavily stained, travel luggage and handbags of coarse leather are washed with a leather detergent while paying close attention to the instruction manual. Stains are removed with an eraser for coarse leather. Oil and fatty stains are removed with a fat-absorbing spray. For waterproofing, a special product for coarse leather is used.

The refreshing of colors is done as described in the previous chapter on leather bags and suitcases.

Accessories Care

Small leather items and accessories such as wallets, billfolds, and belts are often neglected, although they are grateful for good care as much as large leather wares. They are also cared for in the same way. For stains, a leather cleaner is used that is applied with a sponge or cloth. After drying at room temperature, leather lotion or oil is applied. Leather grease should not be used because such leather wares usually come in contact with one's clothing.

Accessories Care

... with a cloth.

Protect the pages when cleaning leather books.

Use Collonil care with the sponge applicator.

Apply Poliboy leather cleaner to a cloth.

Polish thoroughly with the care.

Massage in evenly and without interruption.

Woly leather balm is suitable—as well ...

Massage in Poliboy leather care ...

... as Kiwi—care for bags.

The magnetic locks are left out.

Care well for the cigarette case on its outside ...

Wallets can be well cared for with Collonil ...

... but don't treat the inside, because ...

... clothing care, which should be distributed to all corners.

... otherwise the cigarettes taste like the care product.

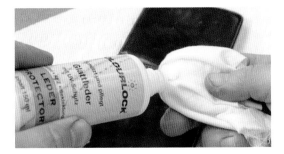

The Colourlock care is gentle ...

Wallets made from aniline leather ...

... and can be massaged in well.

... can be treated with Solitär waterproofing foam.

Accessories Care

Collonil leather clothing care in black ...

Treat the elkskin bag carefully but speedily with ...

... covers chafed edges and scratches ...

... Poliboy leather care.

... very well on brown briefcases ...

Treat tobacco bags of ostrich leather ...

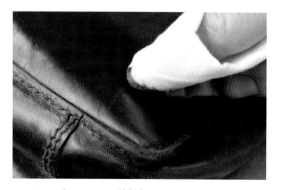

... as can be seen on this image.

... with Poliboy, since it can also be applied to textiles.

Daub the aniline tobacco bag with Tapir care lotion …

Remove the dust of large velour bags.

… and polish.

Spray on cleaning foam and brush the bags.

Roughen the velour tobacco bag and …

Treat the edges with Collonil care.

… waterproof against dirt.

Polish and off you go.

Leather Gloves

Such dirty gloves can be cleaned …

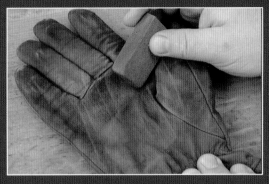

After drying, treat the remaining stains with the eraser …

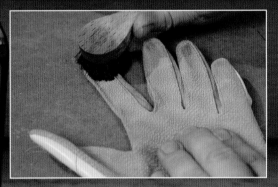

… in the washing machine or with Hey.

… then roughen with the velour brush.

Spray on the leather cleaning foam.

Finally, waterproof well.

Brush the foam on the nubuck gloves.

Wash lambs fleece gloves with the care product for lambs fleece.

Leather Belt

Treat snake leather with care lotion.

... before waterproofing with a spray.

Use colorless products for the white seam.

Care for light-colored belts with neutral agents.

Pedag is suited for the care of belts.

Completely black belts can be treated with black products.

Treat this belt with the brush ...

Leather Wristwatch Band

Soak a cloth with leather cleaner …

… then clean the wrist band well on the inside …

… and outside.

Let it dry completely after cleaning.

Leather Wristwatch Band

First massage in brown cream with a finger.

Polish dyeing shoe cream well

Polish with a cloth.

… for otherwise the blouse will be stained.

Afterwards apply black cream.

Just to be sure, waterproof …

Polish and the wrist band will shine again.

… and treat with Woly beeswax.

Use neutral care for light seams.

Take up leather oil with a fine paint brush.

Treat shark leather with Woly beeswax.

Daub the lizard leather with leather oil.

Crocodile leather is treated with care lotion.

Woly cares and brings gloss to the leather.

Ostrich leather is treated with Woly Shine.

Clean the stingray bracelet with the brush care product.

Every now and then clean the necklace with the ...

... Woly Cleaner, which even dissolves salts.

263

Leather Furniture Care
INTRODUCTION

Leather furniture not only looks pretty but it is also comfortable and, with good care, extremely wear-resistant and durable. Not without a reason today, especially in England, are pieces of leather furniture still in use which are already 200 years old. In addition, they are much more hygienic than upholstered textile furniture because they don't produce any dust, which makes them first choice for allergy sufferers. Thus whoever takes their time with the purchase and searches for good quality, then cares well for the piece of furniture and treats it gently, only has to buy a couch set or TV armchair once in their lifetime. This way the price as well – which for a high-quality set with an armchair can be as high as that for a small car – can be put into perspective. After you have brought yourself to such a purchase, the much higher hurdle is to find a company that can deliver such a quality work. For not only the leather is decisive, but also the upholstery and the base frame of solid wood. Whoever has sat once on such leather furniture and has enjoyed the comfort and durability is not keen on cheap furniture from the discounter anytime soon.

New Smooth Leathers

With leather furniture that is not older than three years, it is sufficient to remove fresh dirt with a leather detergent immediately. For this, apply a mild leather detergent on a sponge or cloth, then rub it over the dirty area and take up the dirt. For more persistent stains and dirt on the leather, use a stronger leather detergent and perhaps a soft brush. Depending on the frequency of use, the leather is treated twice a year with leather lotion or leather oil. For very light-colored leathers, it is recommended to regularly (two to three times a year) use a product for sealing the leather during the first three years in order to avoid transfer of dye from clothing to the leather.

Tip—Thumb Test: A good test to find out whether a piece of leather furniture or a car seat needs care is the thumb test. If the leather can be pressed in with the thumb without creating wrinkles and immediately springs back to its original position after the release of pressure, then the care has been sufficient. But if wrinkles are created and the leather only reluctantly and irregularly moves back to its former position, then it is too dry and urgently needs care. Otherwise cracks will appear soon!

Old Smooth Leather

In case of dirt spread over a wide area or during regular basic cleaning, loose dirt should first be removed with a vacuum cleaner or a soft brush. Then the leather is cleaned with a fluid cleaner or cleaning foam as described previously. Only clean small areas at a time and take up the dirt immediately; don't foam the entire couch. In case the color has to be refreshed, apply petroleum ether with a cloth or sponge after cleaning and de-grease the leather. Afterwards apply the color refresher. Under no circumstances use shoe polish or similar products, which are meant for shoe care; they change the color. For leather furniture there are special color refreshers available.

Larger damage such as cracks or small holes prior to re-dyeing should be ground flat by means of fine abrasive paper or special leather grinding pads. Then the cracks are filled with liquid leather, an ointment-like, synthetic paste. Afterwards dyeing is done and finally the entire leather should be treated with a care product. Care products with UV-filter protect best against drying up.

Be Careful with Leather Grease

Leather grease is only recommended for very dry and brittle leather or for conservation. It should only be applied sparingly and always be applied on a cloth first, never directly. To allow for good absorption, you ought to wait one or two days. Only then should you take off the surplus fat with a dry cloth—before you sit down, because otherwise you'll find the fat on your clothes.

Aniline Leather

Because of the open pores, aniline leather is very sensitive to stains. Fluids are absorbed immediately. Thus the leather needs a treatment with special aniline care products from the very beginning; this treatment ought to be repeated every three months. Prior to the use of aniline care products, an aniline cleaner ought to be used. Aniline leather at best shouldn't come into contact with water at all because it is absorbed immediately and the leather darkens. Stains that have already been absorbed can only be removed at specialized companies. Especially around the armrests and head rests aniline leather easily becomes greasy-looking. If only small areas are involved, special fat-absorbing sprays can be used. But, if the areas are large, again, only a specialized company is able to help. The same is valid in principle for semi-aniline leather, which is only marginally more resistant than aniline leather.

Caution: leather furniture in general should never be exposed to direct sunlight or heaters!

Antique Leather

Cleaning

Antique leathers are mainly used for the production of Chesterfield furniture (Caution! The contrary is not valid. Not all Chesterfield furniture is upholstered with antique leather). It is also used for high-quality leather wares for hunting. By means of the four buttons arranged to form the basic rhombic pattern, the typical folds are created (*capitonné*). These have to be cautiously cleaned with a vacuum cleaner or a soft, slightly moist cloth. In case of much dirt, be sure to use a mild detergent. Be careful! Some Chesterfields are very sensitive to water. Detergents, too, should be checked for color fastness at unobtrusive spots!

Care and Re-dyeing

Antique leathers are generally wear-resistant and robust by nature. For normal care the use of care lotion or leather oil twice a year is sufficient. But after many years of use, the color may rub off at highly-stressed areas, such as the seat base, armrests, and backrest, which shows in a way that only the lighter basic color is visible. These areas can be dyed again with black leather dye. After drying, which can be quickened by means of a hair dryer, the dyed area is slightly ground with abrasive paper—long enough for the color to become identical with the desired hue. For re-dyeing, it is also recommended to test this technique at an unobtrusive spot first. If you don't dare to do this yourself, search for a speciality company and let the leather furniture be treated with a leather sealant, which prevents further abrasion of color.

In addition, and in order to minimize the abrasion of dye, it is recommended to treat the furniture with a leather sealant after the first three years and from then on once a year. After sealing, a "leather protector" is applied or, with glossy leather, leather grease. Because of its re-greasing effect, leather grease should only be applied very thinly. Let it soak in for one or two days, then wipe off the residues with a cloth.

Leather Furniture Care

Put Colourlock dye on a sponge, …

… distribute well and…

… apply it with even strokes to the leather.

Don't be shocked! Here the cleaner is drying.

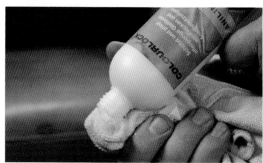

Put Colourlock aniline care on a microfiber cloth, …

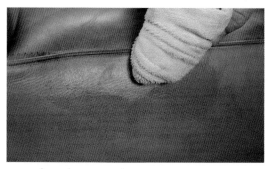

… apply and massage in.

A1 leather care is well suited for car seats and furniture.

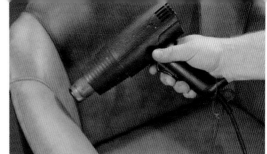

Carefully warm up the leather by means of a hair dryer.

Spray on the Swizöl cleaner ...

Then apply the Swizöl care product on ...

... and clean with the Swizöl pad.

... the warm leather with a cloth.

Poliboy works as well.

Apply the Poliboy care ...

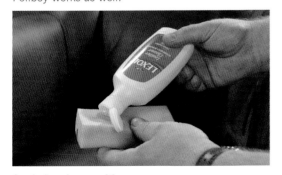

Apply Lexol care with a sponge.

... with a cloth quickly.

Design classics such as this Egg Chair of Arne Jacobsen live by means of their patina. To preserve the patina, treat with Colourlock aniline care spray.

Light leathers are best cared for ...

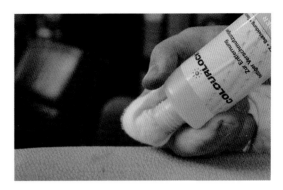

Treat stains with the Colourlock petroleum ether for cleaning ...

... with Colourlock aniline care.

... then spray with Colourlock stain granulate.

Patina leathers are treated with the same ...

Treat light-colored leather with leather cleaner.

... color and with black dye of Grison.

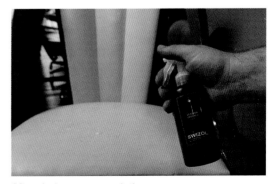

After drying, use care lotion.

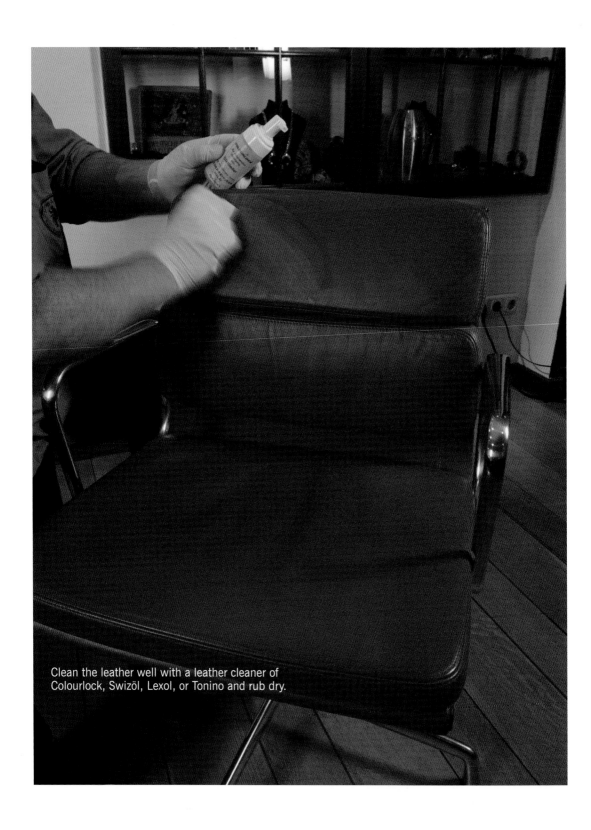

Clean the leather well with a leather cleaner of Colourlock, Swizöl, Lexol, or Tonino and rub dry.

Office Furniture

Office leather furniture not only is highly stressed by friction and sweat, but it also bleaches because of the solar radiation.

To prevent this from happening quickly, the furniture is cared for with a UV-inhibiting care product. Or you can refresh the color by means of a dyeing care product.

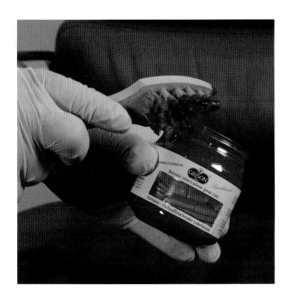

Dr. Wack A1 cares with a UV-blocker.

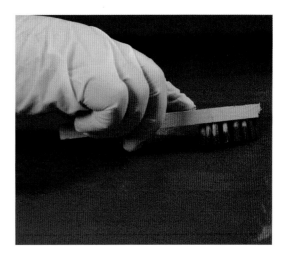

Apply the leather care with a brush.

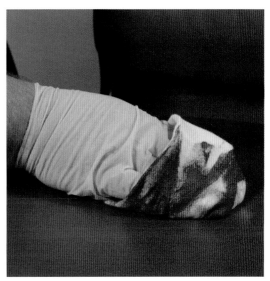

Grisson furniture care is available in several colors.

Polish with a cloth after twenty minutes of drying.

Automobile Leather Care

Nowadays there is no other car furnishing extra that better symbolizes an automobile's value and exclusivity than leather. The pleasant feel, the beautiful look, and, last but not least, the delightful smell make the automobile with extensive, well-cared-for leather furnishing almost irresistible—especially if the other materials you see or touch are made of wood and chromium. At the same time, leather today has to fulfill a multitude of technical qualities: it has to be fade-resistant against UV-light in order to prevent bleaching and discolorations and it has to be as resistant as possible to stains from drinks, food, cigarette ash, sweat, and dirt in general. In addition, it ought to be easy to maintain and its mechanical qualities should allow it to cope with the stress caused by heavy-weight humans. If all these requirements are considered, it is easy to understand that automobile leather needs especially attentive care, all the more so if you also consider the loss of value caused by leather furnishings that are poorly cared for or already broken. Especially with older cars, the residual value can be cut in half quickly because of this. Thus it is self-evident that the leather furnishings should be cared for well from the very beginning. On one hand, you can keep the efforts for regular maintenance small this way, on the other you can enjoy the longest possible lifetime of the leather.

Classic cars have become more and more popular for some time. Whoever owns a classic car usually bought it because of its high emotional value or because he/she wanted to invest money or for a combination of both reasons. Whatever the reason was, especially good care of these automobile gems is of highest importance to allow you to enjoy your hobby as long as possible or to maximize the value of your invested money.

New Cars and Modern Classics

Since thirty years ago, almost all car leathers are chromium-tanned and surface-dyed. To care for these leathers in a way to keep their value and to thus maximize their lifespan, attention should be paid to the right care from the very beginning. Leather that is no older than three years doesn't need special care, because it was treated by the tanner in the optimal way. The biggest problem with such new leathers is the danger of transferring the color of the car occupants' clothing onto the leather, especially with light-colored leathers. Thus, it is recommended to treat the leather within the first three years with a leather sealant; this prevents staining and abrasion. The driver's seat ought to be sealed three to four times a year, depending on the frequency of the automobile's use. Accordingly, the rest of the seats have to be sealed less frequently, about once or twice a year.

Cleaning

Prior to starting with actual care, loose dirt and dust ought to be thoroughly removed from the seats by means of a vacuum cleaner or soft brush because otherwise the leather can be damaged by grinding effects. Dirt is removed with a fluid leather cleaner or a cleaning foam. In general, detergents, care products, and waterproofing agents should not be applied to the leather directly, but by means of a cloth or sponge. But first the compatibility ought to be tested at an inconspicuous spot.

Leather detergents are available in various strengths. To not overly stress the leather, you start with the milder ones and change to the stronger ones if the effect is insufficient. For very resistant dirt or hard-to-reach places, such as folds and clefts, you can be helped along with a soft brush. Only small areas should be cleaned at a time and the loosened dirt ought to be taken up with a cloth immediately.

Care / Protection

On car leathers that are older than three years a care product should be applied after cleaning. Leather dries up by and by, becomes brittle and cracked. Leather care products, regardless of care lotion or leather oil, keep the leather flexible and soft and have a re-greasing effect. Thus the care product should be massaged in and left soaking for several days with the windows open. Then the surplus residues are taken up with a cloth and the leather is polished with another cloth. Here, effort and thoroughness are necessary to prevent the re-greasing agents ending up on the clothing of the car occupants. Thus, also be cautious when dealing with leather grease, especially on the steering wheel. It has a strong re-greasing effect and in general should only be used very sparingly. It is especially appropriate for convertibles, since the leather of convertibles can become wet every once in a while. Especially for convertibles, a care product with integrated UV-protection is suitable; it prevents bleaching of the leather seats.

Tip:

Never use a scouring pad with a hard surface for applying care products!

Vacuum well prior to cleaning.

Distribute the product well with a finger.

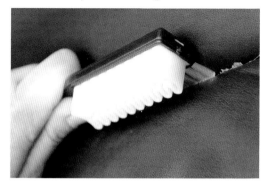

The brush gently takes the dirt out of the grooves.

Apply the care in one go.

Massage in the Swizöl cleaner ...

Cover damage with Collonil cream ...

... with the terry cloth quickly.

... or Colourlock dye.

Soak the terry pad with the Swizöl cleaner.

Automobile Leather Care

Take up dust with the Swizöl Duster.

In a pinch, Kiwi Neutral will also do.

But products such as Lexol are especially …

… suited for automobile leather.

Abrasions can be dyed with cream.

Massage the Lexol cleaner in well and let it dry.

278

Clean stains in the velour with petroleum ether.

Only dab the removing stains.

Roughen again with the velour brush.

279

In general, perforated leather is cared for in the same way as non-perforated leather. But the holes are more sensitive to dirt. To prevent moisture from getting to the inside of the seat through the holes, the cleaning and caring products should only be used very sparingly during the individual steps. Instead, use the cloth or sponge more often on the leather.

Tip: In general, the following is valid: It is better to maintain leather more often with sparing use of care products than to drown leather with products once. This is valid for all leather products.

Caution: Don't use products containing beeswax for automobiles because they can create creaking noises.

Rub into the leather well.

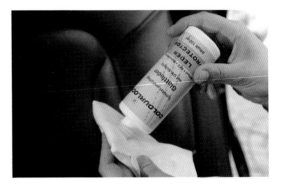

Put Colourlock care lotion on a cloth.

Apply the cleaner generously ...

With grained leather a gray bloom can occur.

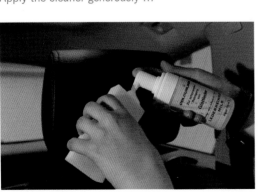

... on a sponge.

In this case, wipe again with a moist cloth.

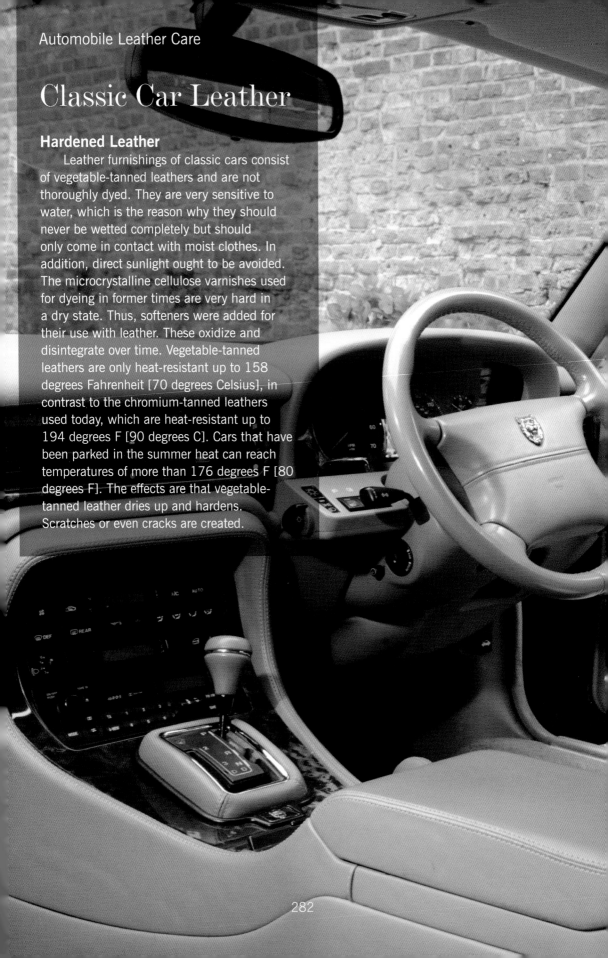

Classic Car Leather

Hardened Leather

Leather furnishings of classic cars consist of vegetable-tanned leathers and are not thoroughly dyed. They are very sensitive to water, which is the reason why they should never be wetted completely but should only come in contact with moist clothes. In addition, direct sunlight ought to be avoided. The microcrystalline cellulose varnishes used for dyeing in former times are very hard in a dry state. Thus, softeners were added for their use with leather. These oxidize and disintegrate over time. Vegetable-tanned leathers are only heat-resistant up to 158 degrees Fahrenheit [70 degrees Celsius], in contrast to the chromium-tanned leathers used today, which are heat-resistant up to 194 degrees F [90 degrees C]. Cars that have been parked in the summer heat can reach temperatures of more than 176 degrees F [80 degrees F]. The effects are that vegetable-tanned leather dries up and hardens. Scratches or even cracks are created.

Classic Car Leather

If hard leather ought to be made soft again, so-called leather softeners come into operation. After the above described cleaning of the leather, which should be moistened with water as little as possible during this process, and after the complete drying, these softeners should be applied with a cloth or sponge. The leather should be rubbed generously with the softener until it is thoroughly moist. When the leather has become dry, the entire process is repeated, if necessary. This can take several days. Afterwards, the leather should be moved slightly by pressing until it becomes soft again. But because of the danger of cracks, it shouldn't be pressed too much.

Shrunk leather can't be brought back to previous size by means of care; this damage is permanent. Nevertheless, shrunk leather should be cared for to avoid worsening this state.

Otherwise, cleaning and caring is the same as for new cars. If a conserving effect is desired when placing the vehicle in storage in a moist garage, leather grease can be applied generously after the use of the care product.

Color Refreshing

Quite often the color of old leather has also suffered, especially the leather of classic cars. For color refreshing, the leather first has to be thoroughly cleaned, as described above. Afterwards all the residues of fat and care products are removed by means of a cloth soaked with petroleum ether. Prepared this way, the dye (e.g., Leather Fresh in the product line Colourlock) can be applied. Here, as above, apply in several thin layers rather than as a single, thick layer.

Similar to cleaning, the dye ought to be applied in smaller areas, from seam to seam. Prior to applying a new layer of dye,

the previous layer should be completely dry. A hair dryer can be used for quicker drying. If the color result is satisfying and the dye has dried entirely, a care product or perhaps some leather grease ought to be applied.

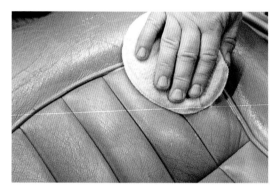

Apply the cleaner with a care pad.

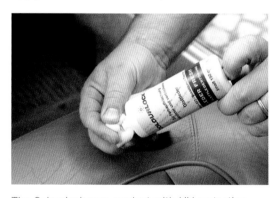

The Colourlock care product with UV-protection ...

... is rubbed in evenly.

Clean the steering wheel well.

... for intermediate care ...

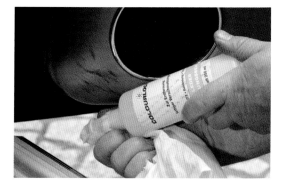
With the petroleum ether of Colourlock ...

... can be stowed in the car in a space-saving way.

... you clean the door of all scuffs made when exiting the car.

The care products of Poliboy ...

Care cloths of Poliboy ...

... also achieve good results.
Finished! Now you can start the engine!

SOURCES

Books:

Berghoff, Mischa. *Auto Care Special*.
    Königswinter: Heel Verlag, 2006.
Ebel, Carl. *The Manufacture of Shoe Polish
    and Floor Wax.* Halle a. d. Saale: Knapp,
    1952.
Himer, Axel. *Bespoke Shoes*. Köln:
    Fackelträger Verlag, 2009.
Kirchdorfer, Franz. *Wax Products, From
    the Chemical Practice.* Augsburg:
    Schuhcremes—Bohnermassen—Kerzen,
    1948.
Leather Care Primer. Rosdorf: Lederzentrum
    GmbH, 2006.
Petzold, Christian. *The Big Book of Car Care.*
    Königswinter: Heel Verlag, 2010.
Prinz von Croy, Albrecht. *Behave Yourself.*
    München: Carl Hanser Verlag, 2006.
Vass, Lázló & Molnár, Magda. *Handmade
    Men's Shoes*. Köln: Könemann-
    Verlagsgesellschaft mbH, 1999.

Magazines:

Shoes Spring/Summer Edition, 1997.

Websites:

www.heinen-leather.de
www.horween.com
www.leder-info.de
www.lederfabrik-rendenbach.de
www.lederpedia.de
www.vdl-web.de
www.wikipedia.de

Shoe care work bench in the shoe department of the Hirmer fashion boutique in Munich, Germany.